P9-BVC-384

The Therapist's Toolbox II

More Techniques for Counseling Children and Adolescents

by Hennie Shore, Senior Editor of *The Child Therapy News*
and Ann L. Rappoport

Plainview, New York

No part of this book may be reproduced or transmitted in any form or by any means, such as electronic or mechanical, including photocopying, recording, or by any information storage and retrieval system without written consent from the publisher.

©1998 Childswork/Childsplay, LLC
A Guidance Channel Company
www.GuidanceChannel.com
1-800-962-1141

All rights reserved.

Printed in the United States of America

ISBN 1-882732-76-6

Contents

Preface

In the first volume of The Therapist's Toolbox, *the editors of*
The Child Therapy News *chose many of the best tried-and-true
techniques for use with specific disorders and issues of childhood,
presented in an accessible, friendly format. This second volume of*
The Therapist's Toolbox *furthers our attempt to gather the most
frequently used and effective short-term techniques in child and
adolescent therapy today.*

*This volume again includes a cross section of techniques. Some are
highly developed and have been empirically validated; others are
innovative and fun. To be included, each intervention had to be
unique and had to show effectiveness in working with specific
childhood and/or adolescent disorders. In selecting the techniques, we
sampled the spectrum of methodologies, from the traditional to the
radically new—and everything in between!*

It is our wish that, together with The Therapist's Toolbox Volume I,
*this volume will become a source that practitioners will turn to
frequently for assistance in their work.*

Hennie Shore & Ann L. Rappoport

Affective Education

Affective education addresses both the child's underlying skill deficits in linking emotions to behavior and the distorted perceptions he or she may bring to problem solving and interpersonal interactions. Through the collaboration between therapist and child, the child becomes involved in identifying the target problems and understanding the therapeutic strategies.

This approach also utilizes games and cartoons to engage the child directly in activities that have personal meaning and application. Pharmacological interventions are occasionally used when necessary at the outset of therapy to stimulate active participation.

When to Use the Technique

Stark, Rouse, and Livingston (1991) emphasize the importance of this approach when children have symptoms of depression. All children can benefit from affective education, although those with behavioral and relationship problems stand to benefit the most when it is used within a program of other relevant therapies.

Each of the games used in affective education challenges the child to provide an example of when he or she experienced the particular emotion, what the child was thinking at that time that may have prompted the feeling, and what the child may have looked like at that time. As sensitivity and awareness develop, the child learns how to read these emotions, possible thoughts, and physical expressions in others.

Case studies demonstrate that through dramatic groups, children can learn many physical behaviors that are also aspects taught in affective education. Improved eye contact, body position, assertive behavior, great dialogue, and more smiles are among the outcomes of a regimen that includes education, modeling, rehearsing, and feedback.

Patient Age and Profile

This technique is often helpful for children from environments where communication skills are weak or undeveloped, as well as for those who may have perceptual or cognitive deficits that interfere with their ability to pick up interpersonal cues. Affective education is used for depression,

| **Definition** |
| Affective education attempts to teach children about the connections between thoughts, emotions, and their physical expression. Appropriate affect plays an important role in improving behavior, communication, and relationships. |

anxiety, impulsivity, and a variety of other problems. This technique can be used with very young children, though not at the same level of sophistication as with older youngsters.

How the Technique Works

This approach teaches the child how to connect thoughts to feelings and behavior through his or her own experiences, not just from listening to the therapist. Stark, Rouse, and Livingston (1991) suggest using five games in affective education: Emotional Vocabulary, Emotional Vocabulary II, Emotion Charades, Emotion Statues, and Emotion Expression. These games teach children to discern different feelings and their intensity, and to recognize the thoughts and physical expressions that generally accompany them. All rely on a deck of "emotion cards," with each card serving as a prompt for activities and discussion. As children become more proficient in describing, recognizing, portraying, and sharing the emotions and the experiences associated with them, they progress through the game hierarchy to more subtle applications.

Affective education is typically part of a larger therapy program that also often includes building new cognitive understanding, coping skills, and self-control procedures.

Indicators/Measures of Success

The effectiveness of affective education can be measured by the child's progress in appreciating emotional and cognitive aspects of behavior. Using this information to gain greater mastery over problems and learning to control behavior would be the next step.

Suggested Readings and Resources

Kendall, Philip, and Lauren Braswell. *Cognitive Behavioral Therapy for Impulsive Children.* New York: The Guilford Press, 1993.

Stark, K., Lawrence Rouse, and Ronald Livingston. "Treatment of Depression During Childhood and Adolescence: Cognitive-Behavioral Procedures for the Individual Family." In P. Kendall, ed. *Child and Adolescent Therapy* (New York: The Guilford Press, 1991).

Anatomical Doll Play

When to Use the Technique

Kenyon-Jump, Burnette, and Robertso (1991) assert, "Given the preponderance of child sexual abuse allegations and the difficulty with medical and primarily verbal assessment strategies, other approaches [such as anatomical dolls] are needed to assist in the assessment of child sexual abuse in young children."

Patient Age and Profile

This intervention is best used with young children who have allegedly been sexually abused.

How the Technique Works

The dolls should be used as an aid in helping the child to verbalize the abuse and should not be a substitute for the child's verbal description. The child is asked either to pick two dolls at a time to represent him- or herself and the alleged offender or to choose one doll at a time. Interviewers are cautioned not to use the word "pretend" or to say, "Let's play like this is you," because such language calls into question issues of fantasy vs. reality and can discredit a child's disclosure. As the child demonstrates the sexual activity, he or she is asked to explain what is happening.

White (1991) recommends asking the following questions about each doll chosen:

1. "Is this a girl or boy doll?" (The idea is to determine whether the child can put a sexual identity on the doll.)

2. "How do you know it is a ___ doll?" (This question is designed to help the interviewer further understand how the child identifies the gender.)

3. "Who is this? Does this doll have a name?" (This question is used to discover whose identity is being imposed on the doll. The interviewer must be very careful not to impose his or her own ideas of who the doll represents to the child. For example, the interviewer should never refer to a male doll as the "daddy doll" unless the child has already done so.)

> ### Definition
>
> Anatomical dolls (dolls having genitalia) are often used to assist young children in describing instances of sexual abuse.

After body parts and functions have been identified, general questions about body contact may be asked, such as, "Have you ever been touched on any part of your body?" "Have you ever touched a part on anybody else's body?" "Have you ever been hurt on any part of your body?"

Finally, the data must be fully evaluated to see how the specifics support the child's answers. The interviewer should then ask whether the child has been touched, hurt, or had anything put into or on his or her body, either nonsexual or sexual.

Indicators/Measures of Success

Interviewers have found that young children are better able to explain what has happened when they do not have to rely on verbal descriptions only. Research on the use of anatomically detailed dolls does tend to suggest that sexually abused children engage with these dolls in a free play situation differently from children who have not been abused.

However, many questions have been raised about whether the dolls are too suggestive, thereby leading children to make false allegations that would never have surfaced without the dolls' use. In response to these concerns, experts recommend that the dolls be used only after the child has given some indication that abuse has occurred, and Kenyon-Jump et al. maintain, "While [the] dolls may be useful in helping a young child to relay his or her sexual victimization, there is not enough evidence to support their use as a diagnostic tool."

The effectiveness of the dolls may be diminished by repeated use. Therefore, the mental health evaluator should be informed as to whether other investigators (police officers, child protective service workers, and other mental health professionals) have used the dolls while interviewing the child in question.

Suggested Readings and Resources

Kenyon-Jump, Rita, M. Michele Burnette, and Malcolm Robertso. "Comparison of Behaviors of Suspected Sexually Abused and Nonsexually Abused Preschool Children Using Anatomical Dolls." *Journal of Psychopathology and Behavioral Assessment*, 13:3, 225-240.

White, Sue. "Using Anatomically Detailed Dolls in Interviewing Preschoolers." In C. Schaefer, K. Gitlin, and A. Sandgrund, eds., *Play Diagnosis and Assessment* (New York: John Wiley & Sons, 1991).

Animal-Assisted Therapy

When to Use the Technique

Children who have trouble interacting in an individual therapy situation can be helped by the presence of a "therapy animal." Animals are often used as therapeutic agents in residential treatment facilities, in foster care situations, with emotionally disturbed children, and with autistic children.

Patient Age and Profile

Children of all ages can benefit from this intervention.

How the Technique Works

As mediators in therapy, pets can serve as reinforcers, socializing catalysts, aids to therapy, co-therapists, pet companions, patient ward mascots, and agents of psychological support. Dogs in particular, because of their interactive, affectionate, nonjudgmental, and social nature, have been effectively utilized as adjunct therapists in the treatment of children and adolescents (Mallon, 1994).

Animal-assisted therapy promotes the idea that it is easier for a child to project "unacceptable" feelings on a pet; that the pet supplies some of a child's need for cuddling, companionship, and unconditional acceptance; and that the pet provides the child patient with an opportunity to feel like "the master of the situation." Animals can teach children behaviors not easily acquired by usual learning techniques, such as social behavior (sharing and responsibility for others) and a capacity to communicate nonverbally. Although children are traditionally thought of as recipients of nurturing and not as nurturers themselves, companion animals can assist in developing appropriate nurturing behaviors. In addition, because animal care is gender-neutral, it can serve as a training ground for the development of nurturance in boys (Mallon, 1992).

It has been suggested that the animal/human therapeutic experience may be seen as having a rippling effect:

- **Patient-to-pet:** The patient accepts the animal and begins to trust it, play with it, care for it, and love it.

Definition

The term animal- or pet-assisted therapy (AAT or PAT) refers to a wide variety of programs that involve using animals to improve the functioning of humans. Benefits may be emotional and/or physical, and a specific program may or may not involve additional types of therapeutic intervention. Cass (1981) defines this documented therapeutic technique as "the introduction of a pet animal into the immediate surroundings of an individual or a group as a medium for interaction and relationships, with the therapeutic purpose of eliciting physical, psychosocial, and emotional interactions and responses that are remedial." Arkow (1993) defines animal-assisted therapy as "a goal-directed intervention in which an animal meeting specific criteria is an integral part of the treatment process."

- **Patient-to-therapist:** The patient begins to accept the therapist as a friend, since it was the therapist who brought the pet into the patient's life.

- **Patient-to-staff:** The patient comes out of withdrawal once the pet has become a conversation piece and catalyst, and interacts with nurses, orderlies, aides, and other therapists.

- **Patient-to-patient:** Other patients are now drawn into the widening circle, as they share the animal's experiences, problems, and love.

Gonski (1985) maintains that the therapist must harbor a belief in and commitment toward the therapeutic use of animals, as well as a genuine affinity for animals and an appreciation of the "transcendental bond" that exists between them and the children. She writes, "A dog and child are not merely 'thrown together,' and subsequently observed for the magic to take place. It requires skill, patience, and sensitivity on the part of the worker to know when, for how long, and under what circumstances a dog should be introduced to a child."

Indicators/Measures of Success

According to Gonski, dogs have helped to facilitate the process of adaptation, problem solving, and tension release. "The ability of the children to develop 'effectance,' [wherein they learn to master a task and realize that they have produced an influence on something] through their interactions with the dogs, enhances their self-esteem and produces a sense of confidence in attempting to master subsequent challenges presented to them through the process of maturation."

"The use of animals with children has the potential to enjoy enormous success provided the project is implemented with discretion, flexibility, and intelligent policy planning. The amplification and execution of additional research studies is also needed in order to refine the technique and to determine the specific value in the casework/therapeutic relationship. Whether the setting is a foster home, residential treatment center, or institution, the canine therapist has certainly demonstrated its clinical worth and has merited a place, along with psychotherapy, play, music, dance, and art therapies, in the field of the healing and helping professions."

Suggested Readings and Resources

Arkow, Phil. *Pet Therapy: A Study and Resource Guide for the Use of Companion Animals in Selected Therapies* (7th ed.). Stratford, NJ: Self-published, 1993.

Cass, Jules. "Pet Facilitated Therapy in Human Health Care." In B. Fogle, ed. *Interrelations Between People and Pets* (Springfield, IL: Charles Thomas, 1981).

Gonski, Yvonne. "The Therapeutic Utilization of Canines in a Child Welfare Setting." *Child and Adolescent Social Work*, 93-105.

Mallon, Gerald. "Utilization of Animals as Therapeutic Adjunct with Children and Youth: A Review of the Literature. *Child & Youth Care Forum*, 21:1, 53-67.

_____. "Some of Our Best Therapists Are Dogs." *Child and Youth Care Forum*, 28:2, 89-101.

Technique

Anxiety Management Training

When to Use the Technique

Children with anxiety disorders, including school phobias, can be helped by using this technique.

Patient Age and Profile

School-aged children through teenagers can be aided through this intervention.

How the Technique Works

The theoretical foundation for AMT is the belief that anxiety or fear responses can themselves be viewed as discriminative stimuli, and that children can be conditioned to effectively remove the stimuli through reciprocal inhibition. Suinn and Richardson (1971) write, "Rather than neutralizing or deconditioning the external stimulus which arouses the anxiety, why not directly attach the anxiety itself; it is not the external stimulus itself that is so much the problem, but the maladaptive and inappropriate anxiety response. Moreover, by focusing on the control of the anxiety arousal, AMT provides the client with a means of dealing with future stimulus events which might precipitate anxiety."

AMT was developed in response to several deficiencies associated with desensitization practices. One involves the time-consuming requirement that anxiety hierarchies must be created for each type of client problem being addressed. Other deficiencies are the relatively long duration of treatment — anywhere from two weeks to several months— and the fact that the therapist must often be present in order for the maladaptive behavior to be removed.

AMT is a partial attempt at preparing the child for coping with future tensions when they arise and might therefore be considered a form of self-control therapy. The training involves (1) using instructions and cues to arouse anxiety responses, and (2) helping the child develop competing responses such as relaxation or feelings of competency. A major difference between AMT and desensitization is that instead of

---

Definition

Anxiety management training (AMT) is a conditioning procedure that aims to reduce anxiety reactions. It involves the arousal of anxiety and the training of the child to react to the anxiety by relaxation or feelings of success. It does not use hierarchies.

being exposed to anxiety hierarchy items, the child is trained to visualize a past event that aroused anxiety.

Indicators/Measures of Success

The signs for a positive therapeutic outcome using AMT are encouraging. Suinn and Richardson treated thirteen students for mathematics anxiety by AMT and eleven by desensitization, and compared them with 119 untreated, nonanxious control subjects. Results showed significant reductions in subjective anxiety for both treatment groups, but not for the control group. The AMT group showed higher post-therapy scores on a performance measure involving mathematical computations than the control group. Although the treatment subjects were not seeking therapy for examination anxiety, self-ratings on test anxiety showed significant decreases in mathematics anxiety following treatment.

AMT is an effective short-term treatment, can serve a wide variety of problem areas without reliance on separate anxiety hierarchy formulas, has a higher efficiency level in terms of client and therapist time utilization, and helps remove existing obstacles to performance by preparing the child for dealing with future difficulties.

Suggested Readings and Resources

Suinn, R., and F. Richardson. "Anxiety Management Training: A Nonspecific Behavior Therapy Program for Anxiety Control." *Behavior Therapy*, 2: 498-510.

Technique

Art Activities for Bereaved Children

When to Use the Technique

This technique is ideal to use with children who have recently lost a parent or sibling, especially those children who may be at risk.

Patient Age and Profile

School-aged children will be most receptive to this intervention.

How the Technique Works

Art activities are easy to use because children love to express themselves through crayons, paper, and clay. One advantage of art activities is that they allow the child to remember the pain in measured amounts and to attend to one aspect of the death at a time. Other benefits may be the sharing of sadness and other feelings with an interested adult and putting some of the inner turmoil a child may be experiencing into words. Worden lists activities the therapist can suggest:

- draw something you worry about;

- draw something that makes you mad;

- draw yourself and write words that describe you;

- draw your favorite memory of your (dead) father/sister/etc.;

- draw a recent dream that you have had;

- draw the ugliest picture you can;

- draw your family;

- draw yourself before your parent/sibling died; draw yourself now;

- draw something that scares you.

When using clay, the counselor can either suggest things to be sculpted, such as telling the child to "create your anger," or let children sculpt on their own in quiet or with music playing in the background.

Definition

Art activities, in addition to other kinds of bereavement interventions, help grieving children facilitate the various tasks of mourning; provide children with acceptable outlets for their feelings, including ways to address their fears and concerns; help children get answers to their questions; help counter misconceptions that children have about death; and make discussions of death a normal part of the child's experience, something that may not be happening at home or in other settings (Worden, 1996).

Indicators/Measures of Success

Children should be encouraged to share their artwork and to talk about it. In a group setting, pictures and clay figures can be shared first with another child, then with a group of four children, and finally with the whole group.

Suggested Readings and Resources

Rosof, B. *The Worst Loss: How Families Heal from the Death of a Child.* New York: Henry Holt, 1994.

Worden, William J. *Children and Grief: When a Parent Dies.* New York: The Guilford Press, 1996.

Technique

Assertiveness Training

When to Use the Technique

Many different kinds of problems result from a child's lack of assertiveness. Weiss, Wolchik, and Katzman (1994) believe that bulimic adolescents do not understand the relationship between anger, assertiveness, and their symptoms. Withdrawn, harassed, aggressive, fearful, and depressed children can all benefit from assertiveness training.

Patient Age and Profile

School-aged children can learn to identify their rights and feelings and distinguish between assertive, aggressive, and passive behaviors in order to protect their needs in appropriate, effective ways.

How the Technique Works

Assertiveness training is usually conducted in context with other therapeutic goals and strategies. It involves having the child identify needs or rights that have not previously been respected and the problems this has generated for the child.

The therapist may demonstrate ways of asserting these rights and needs, then ask the child to role play assertive behaviors. In the case of a five-year-old who became terrified from watching a television horror show, assertiveness training included verbal attacks against pictures of Dracula and ripping up photos and throwing them away (Kellerman, 1980). In the case of an adolescent who felt harassed and rejected by his peers, assertiveness training involved rehearsal and role playing of alternative responses, in combination with cognitive therapy (Selekman, 1997). Bulimics practiced expressing their rights in angry statements and in saying "No," instead of binging (Weiss, Wolchik, and Katzman, 1994).

Indicators/Measures of Success

It takes time to unlearn dysfunctional behaviors and relearn more effective ways to express one's feelings. When the problem is not strongly rooted, some therapists combine assertiveness training with rewards and aversive measures to speed the process along.

Definition

Assertiveness training is designed to help children understand the differences between acting aggressively, acting passively, and standing up for one's rights. It teaches the child awareness of his or her basic rights and empowers the child with assertiveness skills.

Success is indicated by decreasing symptoms and by growth in applying new assertiveness skills to real, problematic situations.

Suggested Readings and Resources

Feindler, Eva, and J. Guttman. "Cognitive-Behavioral Anger Control Training." In Craig LeCroy, *Handbook of Child and Adolescent Treatment Manuals* (New York: Lexington Books, 1994).

Kellerman, J. "Rapid Treatment of Nocturnal Anxiety in Children." *Journal of Behavior Therapy and Experimental Psychiatry*, 44: 9-11. Discussed in Charles Schaefer, Howard Millman, S. Sichel, and Jane Zwilling, eds. *Advances in Therapies for Children*. (San Francisco: Jossey-Bass, 1986).

LeCroy, C. *Handbook of Child and Adolescent Treatment Manuals*. New York: Lexington Books, 1994.

Selekman, Matthew. *Solution-Focused Therapy with Children*. New York: The Guilford Press, 1997.

Stark, Kevin, L. Raffaelle, and A. Reysa. "The Treatment of Depressed Children: A Skills Training Approach to Working with Children and Families." In LeCroy, *op. cit.*

Weiss, L., S. Wolchik, and M. Katzman. "A Treatment Program for Adolescent Bulimics and Binge Eaters." In LeCroy, *op. cit.*

Technique

Attribution Retraining

When to Use the Technique

Attribution retraining has been used successfully with ADHD children, with depressed children and adolescents, and with those who are victims of learned helplessness.

Patient Age and Profile

School-aged children and adolescents are good targets for this intervention.

How the Technique Works

Dweck and Reppucci (1973) have demonstrated that following failure, a certain group of children do not form the response required to succeed, even though they are motivated to and are fully capable of doing so. In their study, they found that those children most likely to give up in the face of failure when compared to more persevering subjects (1) took less personal responsibility for the successes and failures they met with, and (2) to the extent that they did take responsibility, tended to attribute the outcomes of their behavior to ability rather than to effort.

Reid and Borkowski (1987 in Hinshaw and Erhardt, 1991) maintain that attributing success or failure to controllable causes could conceivably enhance motivation and improve performance for ADHD children. Their four-session curriculum links self-control with attribution retraining. Initial sessions focus on antecedent attributions—the child's long-standing and pervasive beliefs about his or her learning ability and performance. Through a structured dialogue with the trainer, the child learns the importance of attributing both success and failure to his or her own effort (which he or she controls) and self-control (which he or she also controls).

In the curriculum, cartoon characters make statements such as, "The teacher doesn't like me," "I am unlucky," "I didn't use the strategy we practiced," and "It was too hard," following failure at a school task. Trainers model use of the controllable effort reattribution following modeled errors. They later make parallel effort attributions ("I did try hard and I did use the strategy") for correct performance.

Definition

In this intervention, children are taught to attribute failure to a lack of effort rather than a lack of ability. Attribution retraining teaches children to take responsibility for failure and to attribute it to insufficient effort, leading to increased persistence in the face of failure.

The latter sessions focus on beliefs related specifically to the child's performance on training tasks. The aim is to instill the link between successful performance on training materials and use of the specific self-control strategies that have just been taught. During the training, trainers capitalize on naturally occurring errors to reinitiate attribution and to promote their attribution to a lack of use of the self-control strategy. Successes are also followed by attributional dialogue.

Indicators/Measures of Success

In Dweck's (1975) study, twelve children with extreme reactions to failure were given intensive, long-term experience with one of two training procedures. It was hypothesized that a procedure that taught the helpless children to take responsibility for failure and to attribute it to a lack of effort would result in unimpaired performance following failure in the criterion situation, but that a procedure providing only success experiences would lead to changes of a lesser magnitude. Results revealed that the subjects in the Success Only group continued to evidence a severe deterioration in performance after failure, while subjects in the Attribution Retraining group maintained or improved their performance. In addition, the subjects in the latter group showed an increase in the degree to which they emphasized insufficient motivation vs. ability as a determinant of failure.

Suggested Readings and Resources

Dweck, Carol. "The Role of Expectations and Attributions in the Alleviation of Learned Helplessness." *Journal of Personality and Social Psychology*, 31:4, 674-685.

Dweck, Carol, and N. Reppucci. "Learned Helplessness and Reinforcement Responsibility in Children." *Journal of Personality and Social Psychology*, 25: 109-116.

Hinshaw, Stephen, and Drew Erhardt. "Attention-deficit Hyperactivity Disorder." In Philip Kendall, ed., *Child & Adolescent Therapy: Cognitive-Behavioral Procedures* (New York: The Guilford Press, 1991).

Reid, M., and J. Borkowski. "Causal Attributions of Hyperactive Children: Implications for Teaching Strategies and Self-Control." *Journal of Educational Psychology*, 79: 296-307.

Technique

Beat the Clock

When to Use the Technique

This game is used in conjunction with other approaches to provide opportunities for positive feedback to children whose behavior typically nets them negative feedback.

Patient Age and Profile

Young school-aged children with impulse problems and/or attention deficit hyperactivity disorder benefit most from use of this technique.

How the Technique Works

The therapist chooses an activity that the child already enjoys—building blocks, coloring, reading, etc.— and ties the child's ability to focus on the activity to concrete rewards. It emphasizes concentration and mastery of a task. The child is to engage in the specified activity for ten minutes without interruption or distraction. Ten poker chips are supplied, and these are subtracted or supplemented, depending upon the child's ability to stay focused on the given activity until the buzzer or alarm on a clock goes off (when the ten minutes are up). Earning fifty chips gives the child the privilege of selecting a prize.

Indicators/Measures of Success

Kaduson suggests that the motivational power of the rewards begins to dwindle as the child's self-esteem grows from having succeeded at a challenging task.

Suggested Readings and Resources

Kaduson, Heidi. "Beat the Clock." In Heidi Kaduson and Charles Schaefer. *101 Favorite Play Therapy Techniques* (Northvale, N.J.: Jason Aronson, 1997).

Definition

Beat the Clock is a technique designed by Heidi Kaduson (1997) to help children who have low self-esteem succeed at a task and enjoy the feeling of achievement.

Bereavement Therapy Activities

When to Use the Technique

The loss of a significant loved one is traumatic for all children. Therapeutic interventions are particularly needed when:

- communication has not been open and children have not been allowed to integrate their feelings of grief into their lives;

- children have misconceptions about the death; and

- children begin having symptoms or their behaviors change and become problematic.

Patient Age and Profile

Even infants experience grief because of the changes around them and the absence, preoccupation, or stress of a primary caregiver. Anxiety, withdrawal, and/or aggression are among the problems that children experience when trying to cope with grief.

How the Technique Works

Specific techniques chosen will depend on the age/developmental level of the child, the symptoms, and the child's background.

Babies and toddlers need extra cuddling and attention to help them deal successfully with the losses they experience at this time.

Play therapy is recommended for children between the ages of three and eleven. In play and in art activities, children often express feelings they can't verbalize. The child may feel guilt at having "caused" the death, and once this feeling is picked up, it can be dealt with in therapy. The child may feel angry at certain people, including the deceased. The child may be upset by unfinished agendas. Play therapy provides a secure environment in which the child may explore aspects of the death that he or she could not deal with previously.

Adolescents often respond well to peer support groups. Tait and Depta (1994) describe a group of bereaved children (ages seven to eleven) who were given play activities by two co-facilitators. The group setting broke down a sense of isolation and embarrassment and encouraged sharing and mutual comforting.

Definition

Supporting children effectively when they are grieving is crucial and depends upon an understanding of children's developmental stages. Different issues tend to be strongest at certain ages, and activities should be geared to the child's emotional level. Appropriate therapy includes acknowledging the child's own expression and style of grief, accurately answering the child's questions, and providing ongoing opportunities — through play and other interventions—for the child to gain some mastery over the trauma, not only at the time of the death but also throughout later years as the child faces each new developmental milestone.

Loving attention, play therapy, group therapy, and letter-writing are among the techniques most commonly used in bereavement counseling.

One technique that often helps grieving children is to encourage them to write a letter to the deceased person. Even though by the time of therapy it is too late to enclose such a letter in the casket, the letter helps the child verbalize some unsaid feelings and feel closer to the loved one. Helping the child put together a photo album or scrapbook is often suggested.

Indicators/Measures of Success

One measure of success of bereavement activities would be a decrease in the child's symptoms—nightmares, violent outbursts, depression—that had been presenting problems.

However, experts in the grieving process emphasize that a child typically expresses grief in short spurts. It is important to remember that just because a child moves in and out of play does not mean that the child has recovered or is no longer feeling grief.

Suggested Readings and Resources

Cohen, Felice. "Mark and the Paint Brush: How Art Therapy Helped One Little Boy." Austin, Texas: Hogg Foundation for Mental Health, 1971. Discussed in Charles Schaefer and Howard Millman, eds. *Therapies for Children* (San Francisco: Jossey-Bass, 1977).

Landreth, Garry, L. Homeyer, G. Glover, and D. Sweeney. *Play Therapy Interventions with Children's Problems*. Northvale, N.J.: Jason Aronson, 1996.

J. Lord, T. McNeil, and S. Frogge. *Mothers Against Drunk Driving: Helping Children Cope with Death.* 1985. http://www.olympic.net/MADD/madd-09.html

Tait, D., and J. Depta. "Play Therapy Group for Bereaved Children." In *Helping Bereaved Children: A Handbook for Practitioners,* ed. Nancy B. Webb. New York: Guilford, 1994. Discussed in Garry Landreth, L. Homeyer, G. Glover, and D. Sweene, ed. *Play Therapy Interventions with Children's Problems* (Northvale, N.J.: Jason Aronson, 1996).

Biofeedback

When to Use the Technique

Biofeedback should be considered when youngsters can benefit from greater awareness about how their bodies and minds are connected and from gaining mastery over certain problematic physiological responses. This technique addresses a wide range of psychosomatic symptoms, including migraine headaches, anxiety, stuttering, and attention deficits.

Patient Age and Profile

Children of elementary school age and older can benefit from biofeedback.

How the Technique Works

Similarities to computer games help make this technique appealing to children. Sensors attached simultaneously to the child and to auditory and/or visual signals show the child immediate and tiny changes in variables such as body temperature, muscle relaxation, heart rate, and brain wave activity. The therapist works with the youngster to demonstrate how relaxation, pleasant and frightening thoughts, and other stimuli can influence bodily responses. Through practice with electronic feedback (also called a "biocybernetic loop," from Rozensky, 1988), the child learns how to manage his or her own physiological events.

Therapists emphasize the importance of communicating with the child's physician to address medical aspects of the symptoms and medications. They also encourage skills practice outside of the therapy session.

Indicators/Measures of Success

The success of biofeedback would be indicated by the child's greater control over and reduction in symptoms. Obviously these gains would eventually extend beyond therapy sessions into real life situations.

Definition

Biofeedback is a process that uses electronic sensors attached to the body to teach children how to take control of specific physiological responses usually controlled by their involuntary nervous system. There are several different types of biofeedback, relating to what the sensors measure. For example, electroencephalographic (EEG) biofeedback gives information to the child about his or her brain wave activity, and galvanic skin resistance (GSR) biofeedback provides data about the arousal level of the child.

Suggested Readings and Resources

Blanchard, Edward, and Leonard Epstein. *A Biofeedback Primer.* Reading, Massachusetts: Addison-Wesley, 1978.

Rozensky, Ronald. "Biofeedback Training with Children." In Charles Schaefer, ed. *Innovative Interventions in Child and Adolescent Therapy* (New York: John Wiley & Sons, 1988).

The "Columbo" Approach

When to Use the Technique

Selekman suggests that this technique comes in handy when certain "difficult adolescent clients make us feel highly incompetent as therapists." He often applies this approach when he has to deal with court-ordered or school-referred children who deny that they have a problem and with youngsters who have a long history of being bounced from one mental health professional to another.

Patient Age and Profile

Selekman has used this approach with eight-year-olds and with teenagers, but there seems to be no reason why it could not be used with children of all ages.

How the Technique Works

This technique relies on the therapist feigning a role reversal with the child. Instead of coming across as the knowledgeable, prescribing professional, the therapist admits to being overpowered by the case and asks the child for help.

The therapist demonstrates empathy for the child. "It must be a real drag for you to have to go for counseling again," Selekman began one interview. Through requests to the child to help clarify the therapist's confusion, the therapist also sets up opportunities in which the child can acknowledge performing the problem behavior and provide insight about the context and reasons behind it.

This information, of course, is not used by the "Columbo" stand-in to "arrest" the child but is instead used in subsequent therapy to problem-solve.

Indicators/Measures of Success

The main indication of success in this approach is a breakdown in the communications barriers between the child and the therapist. Instead of dancing around a problem denied by the child, a team is formed that can approach the issues in a constructive way.

Definition

The "Columbo" approach, developed by Matthew Selekman (1993), takes its name from the television character who uses a bungling, confused, and friendly demeanor to disarm murder suspects and trick them into cooperating. This technique sets up a relationship between the therapist and a child who is resistant to intervention.

Suggested Readings and Resources

Selekman, Matthew. *Pathways to Change: Brief Therapy Solutions with Difficult Adolescents.* New York: The Guilford Press, 1993.

_____. *Solution-Focused Therapy with Children.* New York: The Guilford Press, 1997.

Technique

Competing Response Training

When to Use the Technique

This technique is effective with most common childhood habits, including nail biting, thumbsucking, stuttering, tics, and hair pulling.

Patient Age and Profile

Children as young as four can benefit from this training technique.

How the Technique Works

Azrin and Nunn (1973) suggest that the competing response (1) be opposite to or incompatible with the habit response; (2) be capable of being maintained for several minutes without seeming unusual to someone who is watching; (3) should not interfere with the child's normal activities; and (4) should increase the child's awareness of the absence of the habit while he or she is performing the competing response. Examples of competing responses include:

- for nail biting, grasping objects;

- for body and head tics, isometrically contracting the muscles opposing the tic movement;

- for stuttering, breathing smoothly while speaking in short phrases;

- for teeth grinding, dropping the jaw and breathing through the mouth;

- for eye squinting, relaxing the face muscles and blinking intentionally;

- for eye blinking and twitching, blinking intentionally and shifting the gaze;

- for nervous throat clearing or coughing, maintaining air flow in breathing;

- for lisping, keeping the tongue at the roof of the mouth and closing the jaw;

- for cheek and lip biting, closing the mouth and jaw;

- for hand or foot tapping, maintaining steady hand or foot pressure.

Definition

An integral part of the habit reversal technique, competing response training typically requires the child to engage in a response that is incompatible with the habit; the habit behavior should not be able to occur when the child is performing the competing response.

Indicators/Measures of Success

Azrin et al. (1980) taught the use of a competing response (grasping and clenching the fist for one to three minutes), parental support for not sucking the thumb, and stimulus identification (determining the conditions under which the behavior occurred) to eighteen parents and children during one one- to two-hour session with telephone follow-up. The immediate results were striking, with 92 percent not sucking the thumb after one week and 89 percent not doing so at a twenty-month follow-up.

Suggested Readings and Resources

Azrin, Nathan, and Gregory R. Nunn. *Habit Control in a Day.* New York: Simon & Schuster, 1973.

Azrin, Nathan, Gregory R. Nunn, and R. Frantz-Renshaw. "Habit Reversal Treatment for Thumbsucking." *Behaviour Research and Therapy,* 18: 395-399.

Schroeder, Carolyn, and Betty Gordon. *Assessment and Treatment of Childhood Problems: A Clinician's Guide.* New York: The Guilford Press, 1991.

Computer Art and Play Therapy

When to Use the Technique

This technique is used like other art-based activities in play therapy, for diagnosis and establishing communication between the therapist and the child; for when treatment requires nonverbal expression before discussion; and for when children need to vent, experience their emotions, and experiment through art therapy. It is almost always an adjunct to a larger therapy program.

Patient Age and Profile

Very young children presenting a wide range of problems, including aggression and withdrawal, can be helped by using this therapeutic technique.

How the Technique Works

There are a number of graphics programs that can excite youngsters. The therapist invites the child to draw or paint something, suggesting to the child that color can be used to express mood. At other times, the therapist can ask the child to create a drawing and then tell a story about it.

The advantages of using computers as an art therapy medium include: (1) programs emphasize expression and require no particular skill; (2) art can easily be saved on a disk or printed out; and (3) there are a wide variety of computer programs that are fun and motivating for children of different ages, including painting programs, make your own book programs, and comic book programs.

Indicators/Measures of Success

The success of computer art combined with play therapy depends on how the therapist is using the technique. It can be assessed on its motivational power, on how useful it is in revealing problems to address in therapy, and on observable changes in a child's behavior.

Definition

Computer art therapy applies the principles of art and play therapy to the medium of personal computers.

Suggested Readings and Resources

Gardner, James. "Nintendo Games." In Charles Schaefer and Donna Cangelosi. *Play Therapy Techniques* (Northvale, N.J.: Jason Aronson, 1997).

Johnson, Richard. "High Tech Play Therapy." In Charles Schaefer and Donna Cangelosi, *op. cit.*, 281-286.

Cooking Therapy

When to Use the Technique

Cooking therapy typically involves at least one significant person with the child or is conducted as a small-group activity. It is used when an activity is indicated as a way of bonding the child with a caregiver, or to establish teamwork and cooperation in a group social process. This technique is also useful for venting anger and aggression (beating batter), cultivating sequencing and other skills, nurturing the child, and providing opportunities for creativity (cookie shapes, decorating).

Patient Age and Profile

Safety concerns seem to suggest that this technique is best used with school-aged children. Children with problematic relationships and low self-esteem are those targeted in the literature.

How the Technique Works

Food plays a metaphorical, as well as a physical, role in child development. It is associated with caring, nurturing, denial and indulgence, and a range of social interactions and life-cycle events. When cooking is used as a therapeutic activity, partners and recipes are selected with particular goals in mind. One goal might be to set up bonding opportunities between the parent and child that were missed at earlier stages. In another situation, cooking could be employed to help a child practice working sequentially through small tasks in a larger context in order to produce concrete success. Other examples might explore cooking as a physical or creative medium for expression.

Indicators/Measures of Success

Success will depend upon the specific objectives of the session. Did communication and warmth develop in the interactions between parent and child? Did the child gain a sense of achievement from the process? What group dynamics resulted?

Suggested Readings and Resources

McMahon, Linnet. *The Handbook of Play Therapy.* London: Routledge, 1992.

> ### Definition
>
> Cooking can be used therapeutically to accomplish a number of objectives, including to (re)build relationships, to express artistic or aggressive feelings, and to foster a sense of achievement.

Co-Therapy Using Clients

When to Use the Technique

This technique is used to bring fresh insight to a problem. It can also bring additional teammates into the therapy whose participation may help reinforce ongoing efforts. It is particularly helpful when the problems are long-standing, when a succession of therapists have failed to achieve progress, or when the family members appear to be at an impasse.

Patient Age and Profile

Children above the age of four can be used as co-therapists in helping to resolve problems that affect them directly or in helping with a friend who has a problem. As asthmatic ten-year-old brought into therapy for emotional problems was "consulted" by the therapist for advice on how to help her mother worry less about her (Selekman, 1997). The friends of an adolescent with a drug abuse problem were brought in as co-therapists to help the youth "stay straight" (Selekman, 1993).

How the Technique Works

This is a solution-oriented approach. It capitalizes on the strengths that the child has as a member of a family group or in having built a meaningful relationship with someone outside the family—and sometimes both. It builds on the perceptiveness of the child and on the experience and influence of the other people in the significant relationships. Those voices and suggestions are actively solicited, discussed, and implemented. For example, Selekman suggests "working the other side of the fence" by the asking the youngster, "How can I be helpful to you?" Another approach might be to ask the adolescent what he or she thinks other therapists "missed" about the problem, and what advice he or she would give to the therapist. This is such a contrast to the typical or expected "shoulds" that the child has resisted in the past that it often brings out very useful stories and background information. The therapist can then use this information to better negotiate new behaviors and strategies.

Definition

Co-therapy using clients (Selekman, 1997) is a technique that gives children a "voice" in the process of therapy. Selekman includes children in family therapy and involves friends/peers in the treatment of challenging adolescents and teens. This approach respects the child as an "expert consultant," whose ideas are used by the therapist to provide background and suggest possible solutions to ongoing problems.

Indicators/Measures of Success

There are additional parties who have a stake in the success of this solution, and this may be a factor in how it plays out. Often new information is shared—or heard—and this in itself can be an indication of progress.

Suggested Readings and Resources

Selekman, M. *Pathways to Change: Brief Therapy Solutions with Difficult Adolescents*. New York: The Guilford Press, 1993.

_____. *Solution-Focused Therapy with Children*. New York: The Guilford Press, 1997.

Technique

Covert Conditioning

When to Use the Technique

This technique is used when phobic reactions and unrealistic thoughts about a situation interfere with a child's normal functioning. It is usually used along with other behavior modification techniques.

Patient Age and Profile

Because the child is asked to supply alternative images to a situation, the child must be old enough not only to create new images on request but also to learn to distinguish appropriate images from dysfunctional ones. Cautela (1986) suggests this technique can be used with children who have performance and school phobias, as well as those who fear injections, the dark, or being alone.

How the Technique Works

The fears and expectations of the child are established. The therapist then provides or helps the child provide an alternative set of images, statements, and expectations that are more appropriate and constructive in relating to the feared situation. If the child has great trouble generating and maintaining alternative images, the therapist can provide audio- or videotapes or other aids. The child practices imagining the feared situation and countering with the alternative images. Reinforcement and relaxation are built into the process. Once the less terrifying images or situations are mastered, the child moves up this fear hierarchy.

Indicators/Measures of Success

Success is measured by the child's progress in being able to counter fearful images and situations.

Suggested Readings and Resources

Cautela, Joseph. "Covert Conditioning with Children." *Journal of Behavior Therapy and Experimental Psychiatry*, 13, 209-214. In Charles Schaefer, Howard Millman, Steven Sichel, and Jane Zwilling. *Advances in Therapies for Children* (San Francisco: Jossey-Bass, 1986).

McMullin, Rian. *Handbook of Cognitive Therapy Techniques.* New York: W.W. Norton and Company, 1986.

Definition

Covert conditioning addresses fear-related problems by using a child's imagination as part of the conditioning process to face the targeted situations. The technique attempts to alter the way in which the child perceives the situation.

Covert Sensitization

When to Use the Technique

Deviant and dangerous behaviors—such as fire setting, stealing, or sexual aggression—are typically targeted by this technique. It is often used in combination with the modeling of alternative behaviors and positive reinforcement of those alternatives. Using only positive approaches, though preferred by many therapists to covert sensitization, is not always possible.

Patient Age and Profile

Case studies in the professional literature use covert sensitization with adolescents, but there appears to be no reason to refrain from using the technique on even younger patients.

How the Technique Works

Therapists can build unpleasant associations with the targeted behavior by using videotapes, audiotapes, imaging, scripts, role play, or whatever other means they believe will work with a particular child. In the example of the child who set fires, McGrath, Marshall, and Prior (1979) created five five-minute audiotapes, in which fire-setting behavior put the child in a frightening situation. The tape then offered relief from the anxiety by suggesting to the child how to engage in more appropriate behaviors. This treatment extended over five sessions and was combined with additional, nonpunitive interventions.

Indicators/Measures of Success

One gauge of this technique would be a decline in frequency of the undesirable behavior. McGrath also suggests that if the behavior itself occurs too seldom to be easily measured, collateral behaviors that are related to the problem behavior (stress management, social interactions) can be monitored.

> **Definition**
>
> Covert sensitization links aversive experiences and thoughts to problem behaviors in an attempt to steer the child away from the problem behavior.

Suggested Readings and Resources

Guidry, L. "Use of a Covert Punishing Contingency in Compulsive Stealing." *Journal of Behavior Therapy and Experimental Psychiatry* (1975), 6: 169.

McGrath, P., P. Marshall, and K. Prior. "A Comprehensive Treatment Program for a Fire-Setting Child." *Journal of Behavior Therapy and Experimental Psychiatry* (1979), 10: 69-72.

Mcanulty, Richard, and Henry Adams. "Behavior Therapy with Paraphilic Disorders." In Samuel Turner, Karen Calhoun, and Henry Adams, eds. *Handbook of Clinical Behavior Therapy* (New York: John Wiley & Sons, 1992).

Crisis Intervention Groups

When to Use the Technique

"Normal" responses to "abnormal" events such as natural disasters; explosions; bus, airplane, and train crashes; and random shootings include a range of anxiety reactions related to the stress and associated with the perceived threat to personal and physical safety (Webb, 1996). Crisis intervention groups are designed to help children who experience fear and anxiety as the result of witnessing such events.

Patient Age and Profile

Children of all ages and adolescents who have experienced a crisis or trauma as a group can benefit from this intervention.

How the Technique Works

In any crisis situation, rumors fly. Children are particularly vulnerable to anxiety related to incorrect information or a partial or total lack of information, as adults may feel it necessary to "protect" them by withholding information. When children have experienced a crisis together, the tasks of the leader of a crisis group include:

- *Giving information.* In age-appropriate language, children should be told about what happened and about the efforts to help survivors such as themselves.

- *Encouraging each child to tell his or her own story.* Details and vivid descriptions should be encouraged. The child should be asked questions relating to all five senses: what was heard, smelled, felt, and tasted, in addition to visual memories.

- *Engaging children in play and drawing activities.* Because children have limited ability to articulate their experiences in words, drawing and play activities can be used to help them externalize their feelings. Storytelling and drawings provide the group leader with opportunities to universalize reactions to the crisis so that group members do not feel alone in whatever emotions they are experiencing.

Definition

When a group of children has experienced a crisis, the preferred method of intervention is to conduct a crisis debriefing group. Crisis intervention groups help to facilitate expression of feelings associated with the crisis in order to prevent underlying anxiety from continuing to create any discomforting symptoms.

• *Helping children to identify the strengths resulting from having survived the experience.* Webb asserts that a sense of helplessness is implicit in the circumstances of both natural and human-made disasters. She writes, "Although it would be unrealistic to assure children that they can *always* survive future disasters, it is helpful to assist them in identifying what they have learned from this experience, and even to indicate ways in which they may feel stronger and better prepared to meet frightening experiences in the future."

Indicators/Measures of Success

The group format permits children to offer support to one another even as they identify reactions in other survivors that are similar to their own. The group modality appeals to youngsters, who benefit from a sense of belonging and peer support intrinsic to an effective group. When the above guidelines are followed, group members can have not only improved social interactions but also increased feelings of self-esteem.

Suggested Readings and Resources

Federal Emergency Management Agency. *How to Help Children After a Disaster: A Guidebook for Teachers* (FEMA 219). Washington, DC: Author, 1991.

Federal Emergency Management Agency. *School Intervention After a Disaster* (FEMA 220). Washington, DC: Author, 1991.

Webb, Nancy Boyd. *Social Work Practice with Children.* New York: The Guilford Press, 1996.

Culturagram

When to Use the Technique

This tool is mostly used with culturally diverse families.

Patient Age and Profile

Entire families as well as individual family members can benefit from the use of this tool.

How the Technique Works

The families with which social workers interact usually come from many different cultural backgrounds, and a tool such as the culturagram can assist in understanding each family's unique heritage and belief system. Lum (1992) writes, "Culture should not be viewed as a singular concept, but rather as incorporating 'institutions, language, values, religious ideals, habits of thinking, artistic expressions, and patterns of social and interpersonal relationships.'"

Congress (1994) cautions the social worker not to overgeneralize in terms of racial or ethnic group characteristics. Children of diverse cultures live in homes in which language, beliefs, values, and connections with the community are influenced to varying degrees by the cultural history of their particular family. Congress writes, "Clearly, it is not sufficient to describe one family as Hispanic and another as black while professing sensitivity to cultural differences. A Puerto Rican family that has lived in the United States for 30 years may be very different from a Mexican family that came to the U.S. without legal documentation in the past year."

The following topics are included in a culturagram:

- reasons for immigration;
- length of time in the community;
- legal or undocumented status;
- age at time of immigration;
- language spoken at home and in the community;
- contact with cultural institutions;

> ### Definition
>
> The culturagram is an assessment tool used to understand the unique cultural background, beliefs, and circumstances of culturally diverse families.

- health beliefs;

- holidays and special events;

- impact of crisis events;

- values about family, education, and work.

Webb writes, "Sometimes the children of immigrants serve as interpreters for their parents, thus reversing usual parent-child roles. At other times, the parents' expectations about acceptable child behavior differ from the prevailing norms, and this puts undue pressure on the children, who are caught between two worlds. The culturagram . . . is an essential resource in assessment and intervention with culturally diverse families."

The culturagram allows social workers to:

- understand the complexities of culture as it affects families;

- individualize families beyond cultural generalizations;

- become sensitive to the daily experience of culturally diverse families;

- develop differential assessments of family members;

- involve the family in understanding its own cultural background; and

- discover specific areas for intervention.

Indicators/Measures of Success

There has been concern that social work texts and journals have not focused sufficiently on cultural diversity. With this tool, social workers are able to assess the impact of culture on the family, individualize ethnically similar families, become more empathetic with regard to cultural differences, and empower culturally diverse clients and their families.

Suggested Readings and Resources

Congress, Elaine. "The Use of Culturagrams to Assess and Empower Culturally Diverse Families." *Families in Society,* 75(9): 531-539.

Lum, D. *Social Work Practice and People of Color: A Process-Stage Approach* (2nd ed.). Pacific Grove, CA: Brooks Cole, 1992.

Webb, Nancy Boyd. *Social Work Practice with Children.* New York: The Guilford Press, 1996.

The Dialogic Reading Technique

When to Use the Technique

This technique is effective with children who have communication problems and developmental language disorders.

Patient Age and Profile

This intervention is most often used with preschoolers.

How the Technique Works

Whitehurst et al. (1988) assert that picture book reading during story time offers a potentially rich opportunity for young children to learn language. In addition to being a setting in which children are prone to talk, story time with picture books also appears to evoke tutorial behavior from the parent. Picture book reading is an activity that parents approach with an intent to teach language to their young children and in so doing use techniques such as asking questions, giving feedback, and gearing questions to the developmental level of the child.

In this intervention, parents are instructed to begin with simple questions about the characters, objects, and actions shown in the pictures and slowly move into open-ended questions, such as, "What's happening on this page?" Three general principles are employed:

1. The use of evocative techniques by the parent to encourage the child to talk about pictured materials; this is preferable to techniques that place the child in a more passive role.

2. The use of feedback, which should be highly informative and incorporate expansions and corrective modeling and highlight differences between what the child has said and what he or she might have said.

3. The encouragement of progressive change that is appropriate to the child's level of ability. For example, a child should indicate knowledge of the names of the objects and characters in the book before the parent attempts to evoke talk about attributes and relations.

Definition

This simple technique teaches parents to use picture books to enhance children's spoken (expressive) language skills. It is designed so that the roles during picture book reading are reversed to allow the child to gradually become the teller of the story and the parent to become an active listener, prompting and rewarding the child's efforts to talk.

Indicators/Measures of Success

Reading to young children can have appreciable effects on language development. Whitehurst et al. note that active responding on the part of the child in reading with a parent is important and assert that "this hypothesis is in line with research demonstrating that the opportunity to make responses may be critical for children in remedial intervention efforts."

In the authors' 1988 study, in three to four thirty-minute sessions per week, expressive language development was significantly enhanced for treatment participants compared to control children who were read to in their parents' regular reading style, and the gains were maintained at nine-month follow-up. Although this program was initially evaluated only for children with normal language development, the effects have been largely replicated in a sample of language-delayed, low socioeconomic status Mexican children in a day-care setting (Valdez-Menchaca and Whitehurst, 1992).

Suggested Readings and Resources

Lyman, Robert, and Toni Hembree-Kigin. *Mental Health Interventions with Preschool Children.* New York: Plenum Press, 1994.

Valdez-Menchaca, M., and G. Whitehurst. "Accelerating Language Development through Picture Book Reading: A Systematic Extension to Mexican Day Care. *Developmental Psychology,* 28: 1106-1114.

Whitehurst, G., F. Falco, C. Lonigan, J. Fischel, B. DeBaryshe, M. Valdez-Menchaca, and M. Caulfield. "Accelerating Language Development through Picture Book Reading." *Developmental Psychology,* 24:4, 552-559.

Differential Reinforcement

When to Use the Technique

DRO has been used to reduce and eliminate a wide range of aggressive and disruptive behaviors as well as nonviolent problems such as swearing, school phobia, and thumbsucking. Inappropriate food consumption by two children with Prader-Willi syndrome was controlled using DRO. The technique addresses both individual and group needs.

Patient Age and Profile

Case studies focus primarily on children over the age of five, many (but not all) of whom have mental retardation and/or behavior disorders.

How the Technique Works

DRO shares its underlying principles with well-known positive reinforcement and token economy techniques [see pages 178-179]. However, instead of attempting to increase the target behavior, DRO works to decrease instances of it and its duration.

Therapists or teachers identify baseline frequency of the behavior and determine the time interval for which the child will be rewarded for the nonoccurrence of that behavior. Tokens and reinforcers are administered according to a schedule designed to show gradual improvement and eventual extinction of the behavior.

Some practitioners distinguish between differential reinforcement for other behaviors and differential reinforcement of low rates (DRL). The latter acknowledges smaller increments in the desired direction without necessarily expecting that the behavior will be totally extinguished.

Both DRO and DRL are nonpunitive interventions.

Indicators/Measures of Success

Decrease in frequency of the unwanted behavior is a measurable indicator of progress.

Parental participation in the administration of the technique in the home setting is sometimes effective in generalizing and maintaining any gains achieved by interventions in the therapeutic setting.

Definition

Differential reinforcement of other behaviors (DRO) is a reward strategy that reinforces a child when he or she is not engaging in undesirable behaviors.

Suggested Readings and Resources

Epstein, M., A. Repp, and D. Cullinan. "Decreasing 'Obscene' Language of Behaviorally Disordered Children Through the Use of a DRL Schedule." *Psychology in the Schools*, 15(3): 419-423.

Gresham, F., and R. Nagle. "Treating School Phobia Using Behavioral Consultation: A Case Study." *School Psychology Review*, 10: 104-107.

Kazdin, Alan. *Treatment of Antisocial Behavior in Children and Adolescents.* Homewood, Illinois: The Dorsey Press, 1985.

Lowitz, G., and M. Suib. "Generalized Control of Persistent Thumbsucking by Differential Reinforcement of Other Behaviors." *Journal of Behavior Therapy and Experimental Psychiatry,* 9 343-346.

Page, T., J. Finney, J. Parrish, and B. Iwata. "Assessment and Reduction of Food Stealing in Prader-Willi Children." *Applied Research in Mental Retardation,* 4: 219-228.

Schaefer, Charles, Howard Millman, Steven Sichel, and Jane Zwilling, eds. *Advances in Therapies for Children* (San Francisco: Jossey-Bass, 1986).

The "Disposable Camera" Technique

When to Use the Technique

Cook explains that photos taken by others often limit a child's understanding of his or her own reality. Providing a child with a disposable camera gives that child power to create a pictorial description that feels more valid and over which the child has more ownership. This technique may be applied to children whose circumstances have uprooted them or when children need a greater sense of empowerment.

Patient Age and Profile

This technique is often used with children who are in adoptive or foster care situations and who are having a difficult time establishing an identity and assuming control over their lives.

How the Technique Works

The therapist invites the child to develop an album depicting the people, events, and activities that are significant to that child. It begins with a shot of the child in surroundings that he or she feels represent something valued. The child is responsible for returning the camera at the next session. The therapist takes responsibility for developing the film. Caregivers are informed so that they can cooperate with this effort.

The child's centrality in the album promotes self-esteem, and the narrative he or she creates to accompany the photos helps define issues for discussion and therapy.

Indicators/Measures of Success

The success of this technique can be measured by gains in the child's sense of efficacy and by the utility of this album in helping the child to identify an acceptable past upon which a future can be built.

Suggested Readings and Resources

Cook, J. "The Disposable Camera Technique." In Heidi Kaduson and Charles Schaefer, eds. *101 Favorite Play Therapy Techniques* (Northvale, N.J.: Jason Aronson, 1997).

> **Definition**
>
> The "disposable camera" technique, as described by Jo Ann Cook (1997), broadens the child's ability to create a record that has specific meaning to him or her.

Dry Bed Training

When to Use the Technique

This technique is used with children who frequently wet their bed.

Patient Age and Profile

Children aged five and older may be helped through this intervention.

How the Technique Works

Dry bed training is begun by providing an overview of the procedure to the child and adults. The success of the treatment is heavily dependent on the parents' receiving adequate supervision by a qualified professional. The general protocol, as described by Walker et al. (1989), is as follows:

On the first night, the parents and child review all aspects of the procedure. An hour before bedtime, the child is given a favorite drink, and a urine alarm is placed in the child's bed or underpants. The child then performs twenty trials of positive practice: he or she lies on the bed, counts to fifty, goes to the bathroom, and returns to the bed. The child is encouraged to appreciate how comfortable the dry bed is.

Just before retiring, the child attempts to drink more fluids and repeats the training instructions to the parents. Every hour during the night, the parents gently awaken the child and prompt him or her to go to the bathroom. At the bathroom door, the child is asked whether he or she can retain urine for another hour. If so, the child is praised for control and returned to the bed without voiding. If not, the child urinates in the toilet, is praised for the correct toileting, and returns to bed. In the bedroom, the parents call the child's attention to the dry sheets and praise the child for a dry bed. The child is given more fluids to drink and then goes back to sleep for another hour.

If a wetting accident occurs, parents shut off the alarm, wake the child, express mild displeasure, and rush the child to the bathroom to complete urination. The child then performs cleanliness training by changing pajamas, removing wet sheets, cleaning the mattress, getting clean sheets, remaking the bed, and appropriately disposing of the soiled linens. The child then performs twenty trials of positive practice as described above.

Definition

Developed by Azrin, Sneed, and Foxx (1974), dry bed training (DBT) is a multidimensional approach to treating enuresis (bedwetting) that uses operant conditioning principles to teach the child the responses necessary for remaining dry at night. Positive reinforcement for inhibiting urination, retention control training, positive practice, nighttime awakening, mild punishment, full cleanliness training, negative reinforcement, family encouragement, and a urine alarm are all incorporated into this procedure.

Following the evening of intensive training, the post-training phase begins. In this second phase, the urine alarm is again utilized, but encouraging fluid intake is discontinued. If the child has a dry night, he or she is praised throughout the next day for this success. Significant others (grandparents, favorite relatives, etc.) are encouraged to praise the child as well. If an accident occurs during the night, twenty positive practices are performed prior to bedtime the next night. Just before the parents retire (11 P.M. to midnight), they awaken the child and encourage him or her to urinate. After each dry night, the child is awakened a half hour earlier on the following evening. This phase ends when the child achieves dryness for seven consecutive nights.

In the final phase of training, the urine alarm and periodic awakening are discontinued. The child's bed should be inspected each morning by the parents. If a wetting accident has occurred during the night, the child is to change and remake the bed immediately. That evening, twenty trials of positive practice are performed. If two accidents occur in the same week, the second phase of training should be reinstituted until seven consecutive dry nights are achieved again.

Various combinations of the aforementioned techniques have been attempted to determine which components of the program contributed to its success. Full spectrum home training (FSHT) is similar to DBT in that it is a multicomponent behavioral treatment for primary enuresis that includes urine alarm training, cleanliness training, retention control training, and overlearning.

Indicators/Measures of Success

When DBT was first evaluated, all of the twenty-four children in the initial study achieved the fourteen-day dryness criterion set by the authors, and none were reported to have relapsed at the six-month follow-up. Subsequent evaluations have yielded encouraging but less impressive results. Lyman and Hembree-Kigin (1994) assert that DBT appears to add to the effectiveness of the urine alarm but to have limited usefulness when used without the alarm.

Suggested Readings and Resources

Azrin, Nathan, T. Sneed, and R. Foxx. "Dry-bed Training: Rapid Elimination of Childhood Enuresis." *Behaviour Research and Therapy,* 12: 147-156.

Lyman, Robert, and Toni Hembree-Kigin. *Mental Health Interventions with Preschool Children.* New York: Plenum Press, 1994.

Walker, Eugene C., Mary Kenning, and Jan Faust-Campanile. "Enuresis and Encopresis." In E. Mash and R. Barkley, eds. *Treatment of Childhood Disorders* (New York: The Guilford Press, 1989).

Technique

Ecosystemic Play Therapy

When to Use the Technique

This approach is useful when behavior problems suggest that a child's needs are not being met or when the child's perception of, or adaptation to, his or her environment does not reflect appropriate development and growth. One objective in ecosystemic play therapy is to alter the child's understanding of options in a situation.

Patient Age and Profile

O'Connor and Ammen present case studies of children as young as two and applies the therapy across the entire range of psychological problems and learning deficits.

How the Technique Works

The child is seen as both an actor and a spectator, and interventions therefore have experiential, cognitive, and symbolic dimensions.

The ecosystem includes the child's own physical body and perceptual screen, interpersonal relationships, and representational systems. Structured play combines physical activity, often within a relationship situation, together with some verbal interpretation.

For example, a four-year-old boy became severely withdrawn after his mother disengaged in his care due to her clinical depression. As part of the therapy, O'Connor brought mother and son together in a game in which each took turns pretending to mold the other into various forms, as if using modeling clay. Although it also encouraged reconnection and touch, the play and verbal cues really focused on the deeper aspects of their relationship.

Ecosystemic play therapy often tries to give the child a different perspective concerning the problem situation and encourages him or her to try new problem-solving strategies.

Indicators/Measures of Success

O'Connor views success as optimizing the child's functioning in the context of his or her own ecosystem. One can evaluate specific

Definition

Ecosystemic play therapy is a hybrid model developed by O'Connor and Ammen (1997). It views the child as embedded in "multiple systems," all of which are considered in conceptualizing the problem and making up treatment plans. The primary goal of this model is to help children behave in ways that facilitate getting their needs met without causing conflicts with others who are trying to do the same.

interventions on how useful they are in helping the child meet his or her needs without interfering with others in trying to meet their needs, and also on how effective they are in making positive changes in the child's experiences.

Suggested Readings and Resources

O'Connor, Kevin J., and Sue Ammen. *Play Therapy Treatment: The Ecosystemic Model and Workbook.* San Diego: Academic Press, 1997.

Technique

Environmental Modification in the Classroom

When to Use the Technique

Scarlett and Myers (1998) emphasize the preventative aspects of careful environmental design. They maintain that an appropriately organized classroom orients children, avoids frustration, and helps them become self-directed, thereby anticipating potential trouble spots and eliminating likely behavior problems.

Patient Age and Profile

This intervention is especially effective in classrooms with young children, who have not yet developed internal controls to cope with separation, distraction, transitions, and waiting.

How the Technique Works

Environmental modification includes organizing time, program, and "architecture" in ways that keep youngsters oriented, secure, involved, and empowered.

For example, a classroom that supports children in their arrival and transitions from activity to activity helps them understand and follow the daily schedule. Materials are prepared in advance and are set up to avoid disappointment and to match the children's level of ability. The physical layout of the room (modified open) allows for what Scarlett and Myers call "well-defined activity pockets" for small groups, while meeting areas assure appropriate visual focus and comfortable seating. Traffic patterns are designed to avoid temptations and interruptions. Storage areas encourage child-directed initiatives, easy access, and easy clean-up. Retreat areas are pleasant, safe, and easily accessible.

Indicators/Measures of Success

The successfully designed classroom environment prevents behavior problems that develop around predictable issues such as transitions and promotes the development of self-control among children.

Suggested Readings and Resources

Scarlett, W. George, and Kim Myers. "Programming, the Physical Environment and Behavior Problems." In W. George Scarlett, ed. *Trouble in the Classroom* (San Francisco: Jossey-Bass, 1998).

Definition

Conscious decisions about the physical and academic environment of the classroom contribute to the way children interact, cope, and respond to learning objectives. Observation and subsequent modification of time and space can help prevent problem behaviors and teach children to better manage themselves.

Exposure Therapy

When to Use the Technique

This intervention is highly effective with children who are school phobic, agoraphobic, or experiencing social anxiety as well as other types of simple phobias.

Patient Age and Profile

Children and adolescents of all ages can be helped using this intervention.

How the Technique Works

The underlying assumption of exposure therapy is that phobic anxiety is maintained—it continues and may get more intense—when the child repeatedly avoids the object or situation that elicits the anxiety. Avoidance prevents the child from "unlearning" the association between an object or situation and anxiety. Exposure to such situations, by contrast, gradually habituates the child to it—that is, he or she learns that no real danger is present. Gradually, the anxiety is extinguished. Some therapists believe that the more rapidly such exposure takes place, the more rapidly the phobia will be eliminated.

In treatment, the therapist explains this rationale to the child, outlines the procedure that will be followed, and helps the child to anticipate what his or her reactions are likely to be. The therapist gives assurances that he or she will always be available to help the child cope with the sense of danger and will stop the procedure any time the client seems unable to tolerate it.

The therapist presents the situation to be encountered, mentions any aspects of the situation that are likely to be troubling, and models behavior, using the different approaches in coping with the situation. The therapist then helps the child think through the steps to use when approaching the situation and also helps the child to practice using these steps until he or she feels calmer and is ready to actually engage in the situation. Following the *in vivo* exposure, the child is helped to evaluate his or her performance and to think of a reward.

Definition

Exposure-based treatments are used with children who need to learn to deal with anxiety-provoking situations. Exposure can be conducted through the imagination or by using real situations (in vivo). In gradual exposure, the child and the therapist generate a list of feared situations in a hierarchy from least to most anxiety provoking. The child then approaches each situation sequentially, moving up the hierarchy as anxiety levels permit.

Kendall et al. (1991) report that various *in vivo* situations can be set up in the office, such as taking a math test, giving a speech, reading a poem in front of a small audience or video camera, or introducing oneself to office personnel. Other *in vivo* exposures involve taking the child to a site outside the office, for example, to a cemetery, zoo, or shopping center. Many naturally occurring academic and social situations can be arranged in schools with the help of teachers or school counselors.

In general, children are asked to stay in the situation until their anxiety begins to diminish. With each session, they should be able to tolerate closer and longer confrontations with the threatening object or circumstance.

Kendall et al. write, "Following the first successful *in vivo* exposure, the child often experiences a new sense of competency and more willingly engages in other anxiety-provoking situations. Given the new set of skills that the child can call on if feeling anxious, much of the treatment encourages risk taking. In large part, the therapist also frequently normalizes anxiety, stressing that it is not necessarily abnormal."

In many cases, *in vivo* exposure has replaced other methods that rely on imagined danger and is now considered the treatment of choice by many therapists for simple phobias. Improvements brought about by exposure therapy are generally maintained or even improved upon over time.

Indicators/Measures of Success

Francis and Ollendick (1990) described a case study of the use of gradual *in vivo* exposure to treat an adolescent with generalized social phobia. The sixteen-year-old subject had a long history of school refusal and avoidance of most social situations. She reported intense social-evaluative fears. Treatment was conducted over a three-month period. First, a fear hierarchy was developed, which ranged from least (going to a shopping mall with someone) to most anxiety provoking (going to school alone and staying all day). Items from the hierarchy were used as homework assignments to be practiced between therapy sessions. Tasks were completed in a gradual fashion, with repeated practice for each one. For example, the youngster practiced riding the bus, going to a shopping mall alone, and going to a movie early and waiting in a crowded line. Although she was unable to return to her regular high school, she did attend an alternative school program, obtain her GED, and enroll in a local community college. By the end of treatment, although she still found some social situations anxiety provoking, she no longer engaged in avoidance behaviors.

Suggested Readings and Resources

Francis, Greta, and Deborah Beidel. "Cognitive-Behavioral Psychotherapy." In J. March, ed. *Anxiety Disorders in Children and Adolescents* (New York: The Guilford Press, 1995).

Francis, G., and Thomas Ollendick. "Behavioral Treatment of Social Anxiety." In E. Feindler and G. Kalfus, eds. *Casebook in Adolescent Behavior Therapy* (New York: Springer, 1990).

Kendall, Philip, Tamar Chansky, Michael Freidman, Ray Kim, Elizabeth Kortlander, Frances Sessa, and Lynne Siqueland. "Treating Anxiety Disorders in Children and Adolescents." In Philip Kendall, ed. *Child and Adolescent Therapy: Cognitive-Behavioral Approaches* (New York: The Guilford Press, 1991).

On-line: "The Varieties of Fear." www.hoptechno.com/book48.htm

Technique

Externalization

Definition

Externalization is a process that directs a problem or conflict outward from the child experiencing it, so that the problem is separated from the individual and conceptualized as a concrete enemy that can be challenged. Thus, the child is no longer labeled as "bad" or a "liar" and is offered therapeutic distance that empowers him or her to achieve some control over the problem.

When to Use the Technique

Externalization has been recommended by therapists for a variety of problems, ranging from obsessive compulsive disorder to attention deficit disorder. Practitioners find externalization most helpful when the clients are "stuck" in negativity and feel hopeless about resolving their problem.

Patient Age and Profile

Useful for very young children, for adolescents, and in family therapy, the process facilitates teamwork among the child, family, teachers, and therapist, all of whom align against the problem. Young children are sometimes encouraged to give the problem a nasty or funny nickname.

How the Technique Works

Externalizing a problem defuses some of the blame that the child feels and that undermines his or her self-esteem. Instead of operating as if the child is the villain, externalization allows the disorder or problem to become the villain. This makes the problem easier to identify and combat.

Two steps typically make up the externalization process. The first focuses on understanding how the problem influences the child and affects those with whom he or she interacts. The therapist uses language and questions that cast the child client and his or her supporters all as victims of the outside problem/enemy. The second step identifies examples in which the clients or supporters have been relatively successful in confronting the problem or have at least fought back. This step, also called "restorying," emphasizes the development of competencies and builds a united front with the client to overcome the problem.

Indicators/Measures of Success

Merely engaging actively in this treatment is sometimes a sign of progress, since clients typically enter therapy feeling demoralized and deadlocked. If they can successfully externalize the problem, the therapy team will more consistently focus on attacking the problem itself, instead of being sidetracked by other issues. If externalization works, the team should identify, build upon, and expand the client's repertoire of situations and strategies in which he or she stands up to the problem.

Suggested Readings and Resources

March, John. "An Interview with John March, M.D., Ph.D." In L. Slap-Shelton, Psy.D., ed. *Child Therapy Today* (Plainview, NY: Childswork/Childsplay, 1994).

Selekman, Matthew. *Solution-Focused Therapy with Children.* New York: The Guilford Press, 1997.

White, M. *Re-authoring Lives: Interviews & Essays.* Adelaide, South Australia: Dulwich Centre Publications, 1995.

Technique

Extinction

Definition

Extinction is the breaking of the contingent relationship between a response and its consequence. It involves the withholding or removal of positive reinforcement when undesirable behaviors are present. Extinction procedures are fairly noninvasive and have been demonstrated to be effective in managing a wide range of maladaptive behaviors.

When to Use the Technique

This intervention is effective with children who are obsessive-compulsive, fearful, mentally retarded, prone to self-injury, learning disabled, or who experience recurrent pain.

Patient Age and Profile

Young children benefit most from this technique.

How the Technique Works

Extinction programs often involve the withholding of social contact and attention (i.e., ignoring) if there is reason to believe that these constitute the relevant enforcers of a problem behavior. It is often used in conjunction with other contingency management procedures to eliminate a particular behavior. For example:

- Lovaas and Simmons (1969) found that withholding attention was effective in reducing self-injurious behavior in three retarded girls.

- A child who had obsessive-compulsive disorder was concerned about whether she was going to be sick if she ate something with germs on it. She would eat only if her mother reassured her, over and over again, that the food was not contaminated. An extinction procedure would be to stop the reassurance. If the mother typically reassured the daughter fifty times, the extinction would be to have the mother reassure her daughter fewer and fewer times until the girl knew that her mother wouldn't answer her.

- A girl who was badly burned in an accident experienced recurring nightmares. As part of her treatment, her parents were instructed to totally ignore her nightmares and to allow the girl to spend the entire night alone in her bedroom.

Indicators/Measures of Success

Extinction frequently produces rapid effects, but it can be hard to implement when a child's behavior is bizarre or frequent. A disadvantage of extinction procedures is that they can be quite slow in producing effects and are not appropriate for use with severely disruptive and/or dangerous behaviors.

Suggested Readings and Resources

Poling, A. "Extinction." In Alan Bellack and Michael Hersen, eds. *Dictionary of Behavior Therapy Techniques* (Elmsford, NY: Pergamon, 1985).

Matson, Johnny, ed. *Handbook of Treatment Approaches in Childhood Psychopathology*. New York: Plenum Press, 1988.

Technique

Eye Movement Desensitization and Reprocessing (EMDR)

When to Use the Technique

EMDR is most effective in alleviating symptoms such as those resulting from a natural disaster, a traumatic event, or a specific phobia or fear. It has been used with children who survived but were traumatized by a natural disaster, depressed children who were abandoned by a parent, and mentally retarded children who have nightmares.

Patient Age and Profile

The technique works best with children aged five and older who have a very specific trauma or fear that is the reason for referral.

How the Technique Works

Considered to be a behavioral therapy, the technique is reported to be highly effective in a short amount of time. In beginning a session, the therapist asks the child to think of the previously identified traumatic event or stimulus. The therapist then asks the child to work with the image that comes to mind, making it as detailed as possible and charging it with all the emotions that it evokes. Next, the therapist asks the child to make a self-statement in response to this charged image, such as, "I am going to be swallowed up by the ground," for a child who has been traumatized by an earthquake, or "I am going to be left by my father," for a child who has been traumatized by a divorce.

The child is then asked to evaluate the intensity of the feeling by assigning a number to the paired image and negative self-statement. The image, self-statement, and discomfort rating provide a baseline from which the therapist can act. The therapist might, for example, ask the child to think of the image again and to make a positive self-statement, such as "I am in control," or "I am going to be all right." The felt truth, or validity of this statement, is also rated.

Initially, very low validity ratings (0 or 1 on a 7-point scale) are to be expected. The therapist asks the child to think of the image and to say the negative self-statement while focusing on the therapist's index finger. The therapist moves a finger rapidly from side to side at a distance of 12 to 14 inches from the child's face, spanning a distance of at least 12

Definition

EMDR is a behavioral therapy technique that uses rapid eye movements to alleviate the post-traumatic stress symptoms of children.

inches. The therapist moves the finger at a speed of four side-to-side movements per second for six to twelve seconds. Then the therapist asks the child to stop thinking of the charged image and rest.

When the therapist asks the child to think of the charged image and make the negative self-statement again, he or she requests that the child reconsider the intensity of the feeling that accompanies it. The procedure is repeated, usually at least three times, and sometimes as many as fifteen times, during the session until the intense feelings it initially provoked are also reduced or eliminated. At this point, the child may report that the image has changed. When this happens, the procedure is repeated using the new image until the intense feelings it initially provoked are also reduced or eliminated. When the child indicates that the image no longer provokes intense feelings, the therapist asks the child to recall the positive self-statement and to evaluate its validity once more.

No matter how valid or invalid the child feels the positive self-statement is at this point, the therapist asks him or her to recall the original image and rehearse the positive self-statement. This is repeated until the child regards the positive self-statement as true.

The EMDR technique is typically administered in one fifty-minute session during which one or two images or events are usually considered. When there are several connected charged images, additional EMDR sessions are indicated. The more complex the trauma, the more EMDR sessions are required in order for the therapist and child to accomplish treatment goals.

Indicators/Measures of Success

The EMDR technique is highly controversial. Those who have used it have proved that it works as least as well as other, lengthier techniques used to treat traumas and specific fears. Some therapists speculate that the rapid bilateral eye movement of EMDR works like REM sleep, during which the mind processes and integrates the day's events and memories. Others hypothesize that the rapid eye movements interfere with the habitual neural and affective responses to the traumatic memory or stimulus. Francine Shapiro, the originator of the technique, maintains that a level of relaxation similar to that which occurs during REM sleep may be evoked by EMDR. Skeptics of the technique suggest that the therapeutic effects may be caused by the techniques used alongside the rapid eye movement, which include desensitization, cognitive therapy, and even the "placebo" effect of the therapy itself.

Suggested Readings and Resources

Acierno, R., M. Herson, V. Van Hasselt, G. Tremont., and K. Meuser. "Review of the Validation and Dissemination of Eye-Movement Desensitization and Reprocessing: A Scientific and Ethical Dilemma." *Clinical Psychology Review,* 14:4: 287-299.

Greenwald, R. "Eye Movement Desensitization and Reprocessing (EMDR): An Overview." *Journal of Contemporary Psychotherapy,* 24:1, 15-34.

Pellicer, X. "Eye-movement Desensitization Treatment of a Child's Nightmares: A Case Report." *Journal of Behavior Therapy and Experimental Psychiatry,* 24: 73-75.

Family Preservation

When to Use the Technique

Family preservation is often employed as an alternative to placing children in foster care or adoption programs.

Patient Age and Profile

Children in families that are dealing with a range of problems and experiencing various kinds of crises can benefit from these services.

How the Technique Works

The family preservationist will often spend from ten to twenty hours with the family at the initial stage of the crisis, trying to calm things down. An expert comments, "The difference is that in many jurisdictions, if a case came in at 11:00 at night, such as a teenager arguing with his family, and the family puts him out on the street, and the child has nowhere to go, and the neighbors call up, the typical response would be to pick up the child and put him in a shelter overnight. If [he] can be kept safely at home, that's always better than moving [him] out. The family preservation therapists [go] whenever they are needed."

Typically, in-home family preservation programs focus on the family system as a unit, rather than on the parents or children as individual clients. Intervention focuses on establishing stability within the family system, on assisting the family to identify where it is "stuck," and on facilitating the development of new adaptive styles that will enable the family unit to cope more effectively with similar situations in the future.

When considering in-home care, the focus must be shifted from "treatment," which implies a professional "cure," to coping or managing, which is an ongoing process (Bryce, p. 24). As well, Seelig et al. (1992) caution that in-home treatment programs often represent a "complex therapeutic modality. It requires staff training, a solid clinical structure, intensive supervision and consultation, and an overall agency context that is program-knowledgeable and supportive" (p. 148). But, in spite of methodological limitations in the research, the adoption of intensive family preservation services in child welfare agencies across the country has occurred at an astonishing pace, and much success has been duly

Definition

Family preservation refers to a variety of services directed to families in crisis and wherever there is a child at risk of being removed from the home. It is a crisis intervention, with a professional responding to the situation within twenty-four hours, at any time of the day or night, for as long as it takes to resolve the immediate crisis. The service takes place in the home; unlike other therapies, the family is not expected to come to an office.

noted (Walton et al., 1993).

Often, high-risk families can be enlisted to join together to help one another. Aponte et al. (1991) describe a two-tiered home-based model that consistently includes the community in the treatment model (p. 405). This model combines family therapy and a multifamily community group. Rather than treating a family in isolation, the two-tier model allows the therapist to connect what is happening in three areas—home-based family therapy, multifamily group therapy, and the larger community.

In the first tier, an agency offers home-based family preservation services to families that are at risk of having a child placed outside the home. In the second tier, the agency organizes these client families into multifamily groups. The groups are open, with families able to join and leave as therapeutically indicated. The families participate in groups from their own geographic areas, usually at community buildings such as a YMCA.

Indicators/Measures of Success

The use of intensive family preservation services by child welfare agencies across the country has increased at a very rapid pace, with significant success (Walton et al., 1993). There are many advantages in family preservation. Entry and reentry problems are eliminated, as are the reunification concerns that mark the return of a child in out-of-home care. Parents can learn modeling, teaching, listening, and nurturing skills. Bryce quotes one worker who noted, "The nonverbal communication packed into the one-hour session seems to telescope weeks or even months of effort in a private office." Other family members and members of the community can be enlisted to strengthen and support families as well.

Suggested Readings and Resources

Aponte, H., J. Zarski, C. Bixensteine, and P. Cibik. "Home/Community-Based Services: A Two-Tiered Approach." *American Journal of Orthopsychiatry,* 61:3, 403-408.

Bryce, M., and J. Lloyd, eds. *Treating Families in the Home: An Alternative to Placement.* Springfield, IL: Charles C. Thomas, 1980.

Bryce, M. "Home-based Care: Development and Rationale." In S. Maybanks and M. Bryce, eds. *Home-Based Services for Children and Families: Policy, Practice, and Research.* Springfield, IL: Charles C. Thomas, 1979.

Haapala, David, and Jill Kinney. "Avoiding Out-of-home Placement." In *Criminal Justice and Behavior,* 15:3, 334-348.

Seelig, W., B. Goldman-Hall, and J. Jerrell. "In-home Treatment of Families with Seriously Disturbed Adolescents in Crisis." *Family Process,* 31:2, 135-149.

Walton, E., M. Fraser, R. Lewis, P. Pecora, and W. Walton. "In-home Family-Focused Reunification: An Experimental Study." In *Child Welfare,* LXXII:5: 473-487.

Fear Hierarchy

When to Use the Technique

A fear hierarchy is useful as a picture of the target fears and levels of tolerance a child has for coping with those fears. The tool helps determine the sequence and pace for therapeutic interventions.

Patient Age and Profile

Fear hierarchies can be developed for children as young as three or four who are suffering from severe anxiety, phobia, or trauma.

How the Technique Works

Some of the assessment tools require parental or self-reporting, whereas others are conducted by the therapist through observation. Some focus on behavior avoidance; others measure the intensity of the emotions.

Among the many prepared scales are the:

- Fear Survey Schedule for Children (Revised) (Ollendick, 1983)

- Children's Anxiety Evaluation Form (Hoehn-Saric et al., 1987)

- "State Trait" Anxiety Inventory for Children (Spielberger, 1973)

- Louisville Fear Survey (Miller et al., 1972)

- Fear Thermometer (Walk, 1956; Kelley, 1976)

After the hierarchy is established, there are variations in how therapists use the information in therapy. As a diagnostic tool, the hierarchy is part of the battery of assessments that help guide some therapists in their selection of certain therapies (for example, whether to emphasize relaxation or desensitization). By prioritizing the child's fears, the hierarchy offers therapists a clearer understanding of how to expose the child to the stressful situation in gradual steps. It also provides information about the child's threshold limits.

Indicators/Measures of Success

Therapists should be cautious in equating school phobia with agoraphobia and in depending on adult questionnaires. Assessment of

---

Definition

The fear hierarchy, an assessment tool that can be used for various purposes in therapy, is an enumeration of fears, listed in order of how much anxiety and dysfunction each situation produces for the child. There are many different prepared survey instruments available to help the therapist conduct this inventory.

children's fears should take into account qualitative differences in issues, e.g., fear of getting lost is different from fear of evaluation and performance.

Suggested Readings and Resources

Ammerman, Robert, and Michel Hersen, eds. *Handbook of Behavior Therapy with Children and Adults.* Boston: Allyn and Bacon, 1993.

Hoehn-Saric, E., M. Maisami, and D. Wiegand. "Measurement of Anxiety in Children and Adolescents Using Semistructured Interviews." *Journal of the American Academy of Child and Adolescent Psychiatry,* 26: 541-545.

Kelley, C. "Play Desensitization of Fear of Darkness in Preschool Children." *Behaviour Research and Therapy,* 14: 79-81.

Miller, L., C. Barrett, E. Hampe, and H. Noble. "Revised Anxiety Scales for the Louisville Behavior Check List." *Psychological Reports,* 29: 503-511.

Ollendick, Thomas. "Reliability and Validity of the Revised Fear Survey Schedule for Children." *Behavior Research and Therapy,* 21, 685-692.

Silverman, W., and A. Eisen. "Overanxious Disorder." In Robert Ammerman and M. Hersen, *op. cit.*

Spielberger, Charles. *Manual for the State-Trait Anxiety Inventory for Children.* Palo Alto, CA: Consulting Psychologists Press, 1973.

Filial Therapy

When to Use the Technique

Children with behavior problems, learning disabilities, and conduct disorders have been helped with this technique.

Patient Age and Profile

School-aged children can benefit the most from this technique.

How the Technique Works

Filial therapy was originally conceptualized by Bernard Guerney as a structured treatment program for young children with emotional problems. Using a small group format, parents are trained in the overall principles and methodology of client-centered play therapy. Parent-child play therapy sessions are held regularly in the home, where the parent, rather than a professional, acts as the "therapist," or the therapeutic agent of change. Through didactic instruction, videotapes, and role playing, parents become more sensitive to their children and learn how to create a nonjudgmental, understanding, and accepting environment. Children consequently "feel safe enough to explore other parts of themselves as persons and other ways of relating to their parents" (Landreth, p. 339).

The program always begins with a thirty-minute special play period during which time the parent plays with the child in a consistently empathic (receptive and nonjudgmental) manner. The child begins to view the parent as an "ally" because the parent is trying to understand the child's feelings, reactions, activity, expressions, and point of view. Since the parent does not initiate or direct play activities, the child is allowed to fully express him- or herself. To illustrate, Landreth writes, "The power of this kind of freedom, within appropriate boundaries set by the parent, to direct one's self, to be creative, to be bossy, to be silly, to be somber, to be serious, to just enjoy the fullness of being alive at that moment without any fear of parental rejection or judgment is, without a doubt, the most facilitative, growth enhancing experience that can be created" (pp. 339-340).

Definition

Filial therapy employs parents as therapeutic agents in their children's lives. Parenting is often a difficult, stressful, and frustrating process for even those parents who are skillful and dedicated to the task. When difficulty occurs, and things are not going well, parents are susceptible to self-blame and self-doubt concerning their efficacy. Research has shown that these doubts can have a profound impact on a child's development. However, when parental involvement is enlisted in addressing the child's problems, as it is in filial therapy, such interventions can increase the parents' sense of control as well as change the behavior of their children.

The objectives of the play sessions as stated by Guerney (1969, in Landreth, 1991) include:

1. To break the child's perception or misperception of the parent's feelings, attitudes, or behavior toward him or her.

2. To allow the child to communicate thoughts, needs, and feelings to the parents previously kept from them and often from his or her own awareness. The children's sessions with their parents are thus meant to lift repressions and resolve anxiety-producing internalized conflicts.

3. To bring the child—via incorporation of newly perceived attitudes on the part of the parents—a greater feeling of self-respect, self-worth, and confidence.

Since parents are not expected to completely change their approach in dealing with their children, they are less likely to experience debilitating guilt when they fall back into old patterns of behavior outside the play sessions. What generally occurs, however, is that parents spontaneously use their new skills acquired in the play sessions outside the play sessions and feel encouraged by their own generalized use of empathic responding.

Indicators/Measures of Success

Stover and B. Guerney (1971 in Landreth, 1991) reported that the symptoms and psychosocial adjustment of children of mothers trained in filial therapy improved significantly as rated by their parents. It was concluded that as a result of playroom experiences children were more able to work out their aggressive feelings and to deal more realistically with their mothers in terms of conversation and sharing.

Gilmore (1971 in Landreth, 1991) investigated the use of filial therapy with children who had learning disabilities. He found that through this approach, using parents as therapeutic agents, the children's self-esteem increased significantly.

Glass (1986 in Landreth, 1991) compared parents trained in filial therapy with an untrained control group and found significant differences in favor of the trained parents in showing unconditional love and better awareness of the child's feelings and in a lessening of conflict in the parent-child relationship. Trained parents also showed an increased understanding of the meaning of their children's play. Parents in filial therapy showed more acceptance and respect for children's feelings, recognized their children's need for autonomy, had increased self-esteem, saw their children have increased self-esteem, and developed a greater closeness with their child.

Suggested Readings and Resources

Landreth, Gary. *Play Therapy: The Art of the Relationship.* Muncie, IN: Accelerated Development Inc., 1991.

Schaefer, Charles, and J. Breismeister, eds. *Handbook of Parent Training: Parents as Co-Therapists for Children's Behavior Problems.* New York: John Wiley & Sons, 1989.

Technique

The Five Faces Technique

When to Use the Technique

Claudia Jewett Jarratt devised this technique for use with children who are experiencing grief, but it can be helpful in any situation in which children feel sad, lonely, angry, etc.

Patient Age and Profile

This is an excellent tool to use with young children.

How the Technique Works

A group of children are given crayons and five blank cards. They are asked to draw five different faces representing five different feelings—sad, glad, angry, scared, and lonely. After each child has completed his or her five faces, the cards are shuffled into a face-down pile. Each child gets an opportunity to select a card and then tells the group about an experience that made him or her feel like the feeling portrayed on the card. As an alternative, cards can be shuffled and five cards dealt to each child. When a child gets two cards with the same feeling, he or she tells the group about experiences associated with that feeling.

If the child is confused as to how to draw a particular face, the therapist may ask the child to demonstrate the facial expression used for that feeling and then to draw it, or the therapist may show the child the expression and then have the child draw it.

Jarratt (1994) states that children who have trouble sharing a particular feeling will give clues through their drawings: "Your sad face is hard for me. It looks almost like your happy face. Is that how you look when you're feeling sad?" *Conversions* in a child's drawing may indicate feelings that act as a mask for others. It is not unusual for a child to describe one feeling with the word for another; a very common example is when a child describes something as "boring" when he or she means "lonely" or "painful."

Definition

This activity offers a starting point for children to discuss their feelings.

Indicators/Measures of Success

Even if the child only watches and the therapist does most of the talking and drawing, the child may benefit from learning that feelings and their expression can be safely discussed with this person in this place. The therapist's neutral comments, such as, "Here's what a lot of people do when they have sad feelings [adding tears to the face]. Do you ever look like this?" can be helpful.

Some therapists use the cards as a check-in at the beginning of each session to remind the child that talking about and working with feelings is a primary task. The technique can also be used at home to continue the counseling work. Typical assignments might include the family assigning a time each day to check in with each other about their feelings, perhaps at a meal, where the caregiver can ask, "Did you feel (angry, sad, lonely, etc.) today?" After each person has answered, a second family member initiates a question about another feeling.

Suggested Readings and Resources

Jarratt, Claudia. *Helping Children Cope with Separation and Loss*. Boston: Harvard Common Press, 1994.

Worden, William J. *Children and Grief: When a Parent Dies*. New York: The Guilford Press, 1996.

Technique

Five Things I Do Well

When to Use the Technique

Carolyn Cunningham and Kee Macfarlane, the originators of the technique, designed it for use with children who display sexualized behavior, but it can be effective with most acting-out types of behaviors.

Patient Age and Profile

Children aged five through twelve can benefit from this technique.

How the Technique Works

To help children acknowledge problems, Five Things I Do Well instructs them to list five things they do well (or draw if they are unable to write) on one side of a folded piece of paper. Then they are asked to write five things that they would like to do better on the other side of the paper. The therapist points out that everyone has strengths and weaknesses, and the children are gradually made aware of the process of acknowledging difficulties. Children also learn how strengths balance weaknesses.

The authors suggest that if the child does not acknowledge having problems with physical aggression or sexual behavior, the therapist might point out this omission and wonder aloud why the child "neglected" to list this behavior. At this point, the child might be asked to think of the worst thing that could happen if he or she were to acknowledge the problem. This approach helps the child to identify the source of his or her anxiety. Pearce and Pezzot-Pearce (1997) write, "By empathizing with their fears and then correcting particular distortions (e.g., the therapist will think negatively of a child if he or she becomes aware of the child's behavior) the therapist may help overcome a child's reluctance to explore these issues."

Indicators/Measures of Success

The "test" of the effectiveness of this technique is in the child's acknowledging and discussing his or her externalizing behavior.

Definition

This activity instructs children to focus on five things they do well and five things they would like to do better. The purpose of the exercise is to expose the children's strengths as well as weaknesses.

Suggested Readings and Resources

Cunningham, Carol, and Kee Macfarlane. *When Children Abuse: Group Treatment Strategies for Children with Impulse Control Problems*. Brandon, VT: Safer Society Press, 1991.

Pearce, John, and Terry Pezzot-Pearce. *Psychotherapy with Abused and Neglected Children*. New York: The Guilford Press, 1997.

Technique

The Five-E Method for Eliciting Change

Definition

This intervention is a five-phase method (eliciting, elaborating, expanding, evaluating, and empowering) for utilizing exceptions in working with problems. Once an exception is discovered, the goal is to validate it and help the child and others to "do more of it."

When to Use the Technique

Originators John Murphy and Barry Duncan use this method with children who have school-based problems, but it can be used in any situation where there are behavioral problems.

Patient Age and Profile

Children of any age who are experiencing behavioral problems can be helped through this method.

How the Technique Works

Instead of attempting to resolve problems by focusing mainly on what is deficient or wrong with children, this method builds on what is functional and adaptive about people and their circumstances. It has at its core the solution-focused model (de Shazer, 1991), which suggests that it is often more productive to increase existing successes than it is to eliminate problems.

Murphy and Duncan (1997) assert that even in seemingly dismal situations, exceptions can usually be discovered. The student who "disrupts class constantly" and "never does any schoolwork" has probably behaved appropriately at some time and has probably completed some assignment along the way. Parents who say they have no control over their child have probably been successful in some recent situation. The tasks of the Five-E method include:

Task 1: Eliciting. It is common for people involved in problem situations to view the problem as constant and unchanging. Phrases such as "failing everything *except* science," and "has completed work *only once* this week" provide starting points for building on what is already being done well. Specific questions to elicit information on exceptions include:

• When is the problem absent or less noticeable?

• What is happening that you want to see continue to happen?

• What changes have occurred since this process was begun?

Children and parents should be given "assignments" to take notice of exceptions to the behavior, such as, "Between now and next time we meet, note the things in your life that you would like to see continue," and "Observe when the problem isn't occurring or is just a little better and how you are able to make it that way."

Task 2: Elaborating. Once identified, the exception is elaborated upon by inquiring about related features and circumstances. For example, a child who misbehaves in all classes except math class might be asked:

- In what way is your math class or teacher different from the others?

- How would you rate your interest in math relative to your other classes?

Elaborating on exceptions requires the practitioner to "unfold the noted difference and allow the client to appreciate its significance fully."

Task 3: Expanding. The task now shifts to expanding the exception to other contexts or to a greater frequency. Children can be encouraged to do more of what is already working for them. For example, a child who complained of ongoing arguments with his stepfather was able to determine that he and his stepfather got along better when they talked about sports. The child was encouraged to initiate such a discussion once each day, and his behavior improved.

Task 4: Evaluating. Evaluation is based on the child's perception of his or her goal attainment. Scaling techniques are useful in this task: "On a scale of 1 to 10, with 1 being the worst and 10 the best, how would you rate the problem right now?"

Task 5: Empowering. Once desired changes are made, the goal is to empower and maintain the changes. Questions to be asked include, "What have you been doing differently in math class to make things so much better now than they used to be?" and "What are some of the things that need to happen for you to continue the behavior?"

Indicators/Measures of Success

Murphy and Duncan attribute the success of the Five-E method to (1) the client-centered, competency-oriented view, which fosters a cooperative relationship between child and practitioner; (2) the focus on rapid change, which is beneficial to practitioners who have time constraints; and (3) the realistic goal of achieving small, concrete changes.

Suggested Readings and Resources

de Shazer, Steve. *Putting Difference to Work*. New York: Norton, 1991.

Murphy, John, and Barry Duncan. *Brief Interventions for School Problems*, New York: The Guilford Press, 1997.

Technique

Focusing

Definition

Focusing is a six-step process individuals can use, with or without a therapist, to experience a "body shift" that allows them to physically feel the source of dysfunction and unhappiness. Focusing localizes a physical feeling that has up until that point been inaccessible to the patient. The process releases the body from the tension surrounding a problem and helps the patient feel "unstuck."

When to Use the Technique

Focusing addresses physical feelings that accompany problems but for which analysis, lectures, and other approaches keep dead-ending. Youngsters often can't tap the source of their problem because they don't always know what it is. Yet by recognizing that "we are conscious of only a fragment of what we deeply know," focusing "articulates new subliminal knowing" (Ferguson, 1981). Children can be trained to use focusing outside an office context to address problems as they arise.

Patient Age and Profile

Children who have not been successful in previous therapy, or who seem blocked with particular problems, are those who seem to benefit the most from this approach. Although most of the literature describes focusing with adult patients, therapists do apply the focusing process with children. Examples include school-based distress and subject matter block.

How the Technique Works

Focusing assumes that the problem cannot be figured out intellectually or by using the same methods through which one has already been trying to cope. It is also based on the idea that the body is tuned into the problem but that the child needs to proceed through specified physical steps in order to perceive it constructively. Ferguson suggests that there is a shift in the activity of brain hemispheres from the analytical left brain to the right hemisphere and whole brain; changes in EEG have been noted to accompany "body shifts" that take place during focusing (Gendlin, 1981).

Gendlin describes six "movements" or "subacts" in the process of focusing:

• *Clearing a space.* This step involves relaxation and the directing of attention inward, on wherever the body tends to feel the pain, tension, or discomfort relating to a problem. The patient may close his or her eyes and try to feel what happens inside when the question about what's upsetting him or her in life right now is asked in a gentle tone.

The child is told to just sit there along with the issues for a little while, imagining they are inside boxes in a room, and the child needn't get too close to them. From a distance, the child is encouraged to get a feel for that space.

- *Getting a "felt sense" of the problem.* The individual is encouraged to pick one box and get a general feel for the sense of that problem as a whole package. It is expected that there are many different feelings involved and that the patient will experience "noise" from previous attempts to deal with the problem. But patience in exploring the box from a distance will generate a vague, holistic sense of "all of that."

- *Finding a handle.* This step involves matching the general "felt sense" to a word, phrase, or image. Because many people respond quickly out of habit, Gendlin advises patients to stay with this for some time to make sure the fit is genuine. A small body shift can come with this match.

- *Resonating.* Providing enough time for this step is important. It takes some checking to try out the handle and feel how it captures the body sense. There may be some adjustment. It should not be rushed.

- *Asking.* In case the body shift has not already occurred, this step returns to the felt sense and asks more specifically what it is and how it feels. Prompts include, "What is the worst of this?" and "What would it take for this to feel okay?" Then the child and therapist wait in a supportive, friendly way for the body shift.

- *Receiving.* Patients usually experience relief, parallel to the feeling of having forgotten something and finally recalling what that forgotten item is. However, they are left with unfinished business that remains for resolution. Gendlin (1981) emphasizes the progress that should be celebrated as one has removed the block and suggests that the unfinished issues will be dealt with in due time.

Body wisdom, when listened to and trusted, is the source of change.

Indicators/Measures of Success

Gendlin (1981) acknowledges that uncertainties remain about why the process works. However, case studies indicate that focusing can move patients who have been stuck on problems for long periods of time. Changes in brain waves, after focusing has produced a body shift, suggest that genuine physiological changes can also accompany this change in feelings.

Suggested Readings and Resources

Ferguson, M. "Introduction." In *Focusing*. Eugene Gendlin, Ph.D. (New York: Bantam Books, 1981).

The Focusing Institute: http://www.focusing.org/

Gendlin, Eugene. *Focusing*. New York: Bantam Books, 1981.

McMullin, Rian. *Handbook of Cognitive Therapy Techniques*. New York: W.W. Norton & Company, 1986.

Functional Family Therapy

When to Use the Technique

This therapy was designed specifically for treating juvenile delinquents and their families. It is based on research indicating that families of delinquent children show higher levels of defensiveness and lower levels of mutual support than do families of nondelinquent children (Alexander and Parsons, 1973).

Patient Age and Profile

In addition to juvenile delinquents and aggressive children, adolescents and their families can benefit from FFT.

How the Technique Works

In FFT, families typically receive a total of eight ninety-minute sessions over a four-week period. The main goal of the sessions is to change family interactions and communication patterns to promote more adaptive functioning (Kazdin, 1987). Families are asked to read a manual describing social learning principles and are taught behavioral management strategies, including behavioral contracting and contingency management. Therapists help family members to increase emotional support, to use positive reinforcement, to establish clearer communication, to identify desirable behaviors, to develop constructive negotiations, and to identify solutions to interpersonal problems.

Family members are taught to relabel problems to reduce assigning blame. Direct alteration of family communication patterns is attempted in the treatment sessions, as the therapist provides immediate social reinforcement for solution-oriented statements. Family members are asked to identify desired behaviors for one another and to use a home reinforcement system to promote those behaviors.

Indicators/Measures of Success

Alexander and Parsons (1973) reported that positive family interactions and lower recidivism rates from juvenile court were maintained up to eighteen months after FFT treatment. Delinquents and members of their families who received FFT showed increased family discussions, demonstrated more equalized speaking among themselves, and

Definition

Functional family therapy (FFT) is based on system theory and behaviorism and also includes attention to cognitive processes. It is designed to increase communication and support within families by use of the technique of contingency contracting. Problems are conceptualized according to the functions they serve for the family system and for individual family members.

produced more spontaneous speech than did those who did not receive increased attention or were not in treatment. Family changes of FFT treatment groups were also shown to be greater than those of families in a control group, in client-centered counseling, or in psychodynamic therapy.

In another study Klein, Alexander, and Parsons (1977) demonstrated that the delinquents' siblings show significantly lower rates of referral to juvenile courts more than two years later. Fifteen months after treatment, delinquent adolescents who underwent FFT were less likely to be charged with an offense than were adolescents who received standard mental health services or who were placed in group homes.

Suggested Readings and Resources

Alexander, James, and Bruce Parsons. "Short-Term Behavioral Intervention with Delinquent Families: Impact on Family Process and Recidivism." *Journal of Abnormal Psychology,* 81(3): 219-225.

Christenson, Sandra, Julie Hirsch, and Christine Hurley. "Families with Aggressive Children and Adolescents." In Arnold Goldstein and Jane Conoley, eds. *School Violence Intervention: A Practical Handbook* (New York: The Guilford Press, 1997).

Kazdin, Alan. "Treatment of Antisocial Behavior in Children: Current Status and Future Directions." *Psychological Bulletin,* 102:2, 187-203.

Klein, N., James Alexander, and Bruce Parsons. "Impact of Family Systems Intervention on Recidivism and Sibling Delinquency: A Model of Primary Prevention and Program Evaluation." *Journal of Consulting and Clinical Psychology,* 45: 469-474.

The Garbage Bag Technique

When to Use the Technique

The technique has been used effectively with children who have been abused, maltreated, and/or traumatized by a particular event or series of events.

Patient Age and Profile

Preschoolers through adolescents can benefit from this technique.

How the Technique Works

Beverly James (1989), creator of this exercise, asserts that children are ready to directly acknowledge their feelings, ideas, and behaviors related to traumatizing events once they have learned to identify and express these feelings through indirect clinical work, and once they understand that feelings are not actions. She uses the Garbage Bag technique as a means to accomplish this.

The technique begins with the therapist drawing a parallel between actual pieces of garbage and the strong feelings associated with the traumatic event. The therapist continues by explaining that keeping these feelings and thoughts secret is like carrying a bag of garbage around. The child is encouraged to gradually get rid of each piece of "garbage" [e.g., distressing feelings and ideas about the event(s)]. To aid in this process, the therapist asks the child to identify each aversive or distressing event or episode related to the trauma. The therapist writes each event on a separate piece of paper. The incidents, once written down and "exposed," not only are "contained" by the therapist but also can no longer be successfully repressed. The child is not given the chance to elaborate on the events, but he or she may list aversive events other than the trauma.

The purpose of writing each episode or incident on a separate piece of paper is to divide the maltreatment or trauma into more manageable "bits." The pieces of paper are put into a brown paper bag that symbolically contains the memories and feelings associated with the trauma. Each week the child is invited to reach into the bag and pick out one piece of paper and discuss that particular episode or incident.

> ### Definition
>
> This exercise, which uses the metaphor of a garbage bag, is designed to help uncover the overpowering and aversive feelings following a traumatizing event.

Through disclosure, the child's anxiety is extinguished, and he or she is exposed to particular aspects of the trauma. The child is allowed to throw the paper back into the bag and choose another if he or she is not ready to discuss the first topic, giving the child some sense of control. If the child elects to discuss the first topic chosen, the therapist and child can discuss it directly or choose another method, such as drawing.

Indicators/Measures of Success

If this exercise is effective, the child will more clearly understand why he or she is reviewing the traumatizing event and will gain a sense of accomplishment as each piece is mastered. The technique appears to be most effective when secrecy and shame are involved in what has happened.

James writes, "It is very important to recognize that a child who has learned to substitute expressions of emotion for inhibition has not yet completed the healing process, although his accomplishment is a positive achievement. The child who has gained some control over impulse-ridden behavior is likewise not yet finished with treatment, although he, too, has taken an important, positive step. These changes are insufficient. Children need to *comprehend* what happened to them. They need to explore their ideas and feelings about the event, and talk about their behavioral responses to what happened. Once they grasp the reasons for their thoughts, feelings, and behaviors, they will be better able to understand and accept, emotionally and physically, the realities of what happened to them, and their own participation" (p. 166).

Pearce and Pezzot-Pearce elaborate further. "In the Garbage Bag exercise," they explain, "writing down the aversive or distressing episodes, incidents, or issues puts them into a concrete form to which the child can attach feelings and cognitions… By symbolically emptying the garbage bag of these issues, the child is provided with a concrete reminder that he or she is beginning to master these distressing feelings and is making real progress: the fewer pieces of 'garbage' left in the bag are tangible proof of this progress" (p. 243).

Suggested Readings and Resources

James, Beverly. *Treating Traumatized Children: New Insights and Creative Interventions.* New York: Free Press, 1989.

Pearce, John, and Terry Pezzot-Pearce. *Psychotherapy with Abused and Neglected Children.* New York: The Guilford Press, 1997.

Graphing

When to Use the Technique

Bumpass et al. (1983) use this technique with children who set fires, but it can also be used as part of a treatment plan for most antisocial behaviors. These authors use graphing in addition to treating the child and family with psychodynamically oriented therapy relating to the child's specific psychopathology.

Patient Age and Profile

Children of all ages who are not resistant or opposed to describing events and feelings can be helped through this technique.

How the Technique Works

The authors maintain that the graph, which is a concrete visualization, aids the child's ego in correlating cause-and-effect relationships between feelings and actions. The technique follows several basic steps:

- The child is told that the behavior is the result of feelings, and that once these feelings are recognized, the behavior can be controlled.

- The child then describes the behavior, external stimuli, and feelings in regard to the most recent episode. The therapist constructs the graph according to the child's description. Parents, who are present, are encouraged to make any corrections they think are needed.

- The events are listed across the bottom of the page, and the episode behavior (in this case, fire setting) is placed in the middle of the page.

- Feelings are graphed according to intensity. Each feeling is represented by its own line and is labeled. The graph usually reveals that a sequence of events and feelings resulted in the episode. Common feelings reported are sadness, loneliness, and anger. In fire setting cases, the authors report that children expressed that they felt fearful just prior to and after setting the fire.

- The therapist interprets the graph to the child, and both parents and child verbalize what has been revealed.

- The family and child are asked to discuss how they can break the cycle of events. Understanding that feelings are the part of the cycle

Definition

Graphing, a technique used to treat antisocial disorders, sequentially correlates events, feelings, and behavior. The actual graph consists of a chronological list of the events that preceded and followed an antisocial episode. The goal is to have the child and family see a sequence of precipitating events, reactions, or feelings, and resulting behavior.

that signals the behavior, the child should understand that once the feelings are experienced, he or she can make a choice about behavior. The child is asked to focus on alternative behaviors already used when he or she is not setting fires or engaged in the antisocial behavior.

- At the end of the session, the child is told that he or she probably will not set a fire in the coming week. If the child gets the urge to do so, he or she is encouraged to call the therapist.

- If fire setting occurs, the next session is used to graph the incident, and if it does not, the treatment reverts to traditional psychodynamic therapeutic interviews. Once the child becomes aware of the cause-and-effect relationship between feelings and actions, therapy should focus on underlying factors.

Indicators/Measures of Success

The child's ability to see the cause-and-effect relationship of feelings and actions may be the most important indicator of the success of this technique.

Suggested Readings and Resources

Bumpass, Eugene, Diane F. Fagelman, and Royanna Brix. "Intervention With Children Who Set Fires." *American Journal of Psychotherapy,* 37:3, 328-345.

Group Behavior Rehearsal

When to Use the Technique

This approach is often used in penal and institutional settings with delinquent youth, but it is a useful preventative tool in drug education programs aimed at teaching children to resist the temptation of drugs. Finally, whenever children need to develop problem-solving skills or social withdrawal prevents a youngster from taking the initiative, this technique should be considered.

Patient Age and Profile

Rehearsal groups can be organized for preschoolers. However, care should be taken in selecting appropriate members, keeping in mind the optimum size and the goals of the group.

How the Technique Works

Group work is usually conducted within a broader treatment plan that also includes private sessions. The group rehearsals focus on situations resembling the target problems. Gittleman (1977) gives an example of peer pressure leading to stealing. The group enacts the setting and engages in realistic dialogue, calling the patient "chicken" and challenging or pressuring the patient into stealing. Then the patient practices alternative, appropriate behaviors. Praise and other reinforcements are provided.

Group therapy is thought to be effective because of the motivational impact of peer groups and the notion that social interaction helps overcome alienation and isolation. Rehearsal of behaviors in anticipation of a situation is hoped to increase the chances that the child will respond appropriately.

Indicators/Measures of Success

Cooperation and success in therapy are only part of the objective. The real indication of success would be if the child actually applies to real settings the skills rehearsed in treatment.

Suggested Readings and Resources

Gittleman, Martin. "Behavior Rehearsal with Children in a Community Mental Health Setting." In Charles Schaefer and Howard Millman, eds. *Therapies for Children* (San Francisco: Jossey-Bass, 1977).

Definition

This technique gives members of a group structured opportunities to rehearse a wide range of scenarios pertaining to a variety of interpersonal problems. Based on the hypothesis that "an argument has less persuasive power if one has already heard the counterarguments" (Gittleman, 1977), group behavior rehearsal is a way for at-risk youth to practice encountering troublesome settings and experiment with alternative responses.

Technique

Habit Reversal

When to Use the Technique

Habit reversal was designed for use with most common childhood habits, including nail biting, thumbsucking, stuttering, tics, and hair pulling.

Patient Age and Profile

Children as young as four can be taught this technique.

How the Technique Works

The habit reversal method consists of thirteen components; however, the number, length, and types of sessions needed for successful implementation have varied from a single two-hour session to twelve individual one-hour sessions. The components, all or some of which have been used with a successful outcome, are:

1. **Competing response training.** The child pairs an inconspicuous competing response, such as grasping or clenching the fists, with the habit.

2. **Awareness training.** The child self-observes in a mirror to increase awareness of the specific movements involved in the habit. The habit is performed slowly and deliberately while it is described aloud.

3. **Identifying response precursors and habit-prone situations.** The child identifies situations in which the habit is likely to occur in order to be prepared to use a competing behavior when entering these situations.

4. **Relaxation training.** The child learns a method of relaxation in stressful or habit-promoting situations.

5. **Habit prevention and interruption training.** The competing response is immediately practiced for three minutes whenever the habit might or does occur.

6. **Positive attention overcorrection.** The child practices a positive and related alternative to the habit (such as grooming the nails for a nail-biter).

Definition

In this behavioral method of habit elimination, the child practices movements that are the reverse of the nervous habit, learns to be aware of each instance of the habit and to differentiate it from its usual response chain, and receives social approval for his or her efforts to inhibit the habit.

7. **Daily practice.** The child practices the competing reaction in front of a mirror daily, until it becomes routine behavior, and rehearses the competing response while imagining habit-promoting situations.

8. **Self-recording.** Both impulses and instances of the habit are recorded daily.

9. **Display of improvement.** By entering habit-prone situations, children can display their level of improvement.

10. **Social support.** A significant other is taught positive ways to encourage and remind the child to stop the habit. Parents are instructed to maintain a high ratio of positive statements to reminder statements.

11. **Annoyance/inconvenience review.** The problems caused by the habit are reviewed to increase motivation and to identify sources of reinforcement. Children are asked, "What are the reasons to eliminate the habit?" and "What are the situations in which the habit has caused problems?"

Some of the advantages of habit reversal include:

- *brevity* (with some treatments being performed in one two-hour session);

- *immediacy* (with significant reductions often occurring the first day of treatment);

- *efficacy* (with symptoms being reduced by over 80 percent in most cases);

- *durability* (with treatment gains being maintained at follow-up);

- *flexibility* (with treatment success resulting in some cases whether subjects are treated by a behavior therapist or simply provided with a detailed treatment manual); and

- *consistency* (with similar results being obtained by several independent research groups).

Indicators/Measures of Success

In Wood and Miltenberger's 1996 study, two children with tics were taught to use habit reversal procedures. For one fourteen-year-old boy with a head/shoulder jerking tic, the frequency was reduced from an estimated 8,000 occurrences per day to 12 occurrences per day. A second fourteen-year-old boy with an elbow flapping/shoulder-jerking tic decreased his tic frequency from a self-reported baseline of 150 to zero at three weeks posttreatment.

Suggested Readings and Resources

Azrin, Nathan, and Gregory R. Nunn. "Habit Reversal: A Method of Eliminating Nervous Habits and Tics. *Behavioral Research and Therapy,* 11: 619-628.

Peterson, A., R. Campise, and N. Azrin. "Behavioral and Pharmacological Treatments for Tic and Habit Disorders: A Review." *Developmental and Behavioral Pediatrics,* 15(6): 430-441.

Schaefer, Charles, Howard Millman, Steven Sichel, and Jane Zwilling, eds. "Habit Disorders." In *Advances in Therapies for Children* (San Francisco: Jossey Bass, 1986).

Woods, D., and Raymond Miltenberger. "A Review of Habit Reversal with Childhood Habit Disorders." *Education and Treatment of Children,* 19(2): 197-214.

Hakomi Therapy

When to Use the Technique

This approach was conceived for use with adolescents and adults that have serious emotional disturbances. There are similarities in style and format to Eugene Gendlin's "focusing" approach [see pp. 78 to 80]. Although it was not intended that pieces of the Hakomi approach would be adopted without the entire framework, it is likely that many therapists do use some of the techniques in context with other therapeutic strategies.

Patient Age and Profile

Hakomi Therapy is used with children older than seven, primarily adolescents and adults. These patients present major dysfunctional behaviors in school and relationships, typically a result of problematic relationships with primary caregivers during the child's early development.

How the Technique Works

A transformation in the child's perceptual screen (Hakomi calls this the "core organizing principle") is a goal of this therapy. Certain principles and strategies apply:

- Create trust and safety; empower the child, making no judgments.

- Make "contact" with the child through "Huh?" statements that try to acknowledge or reflect back to the child his or her own reaction to the physical/psychological experience, but allowing for correction and clarification from the child.

- Help the child to access the experiences/feelings that will reach to the core problem. Use right brain questions to help the child "hang out" with the experience and feelings and explore more fully its meaning.

- Help the child process and integrate the pivotal experiences. Appropriately "probe" the "creative" potential of "barriers" by (paradoxically) indulging and supporting the child's defenses, so that he or she will not have to work so hard to maintain them.

Definition

Hakomi Therapy, based on the work of Ronald Kurtz, is a multidimensional approach for treating seriously disturbed adolescents. This approach emphasizes the unity between mind and body and the importance of the child's core organizing beliefs in his or her stimulus-response behaviors. Hakomi views the child holistically, as a total organism reacting in a number of complex environments. The therapist takes a very cautious, nonthreatening, nonjudgmental, nonprescriptive stance in helping the child heal her- or himself. The therapist trusts in the child's "inner wisdom" and capacity for self-correction and encourages the child to explore his or her own experience and grow from it.

Hakomi Therapy discusses different levels of consciousness of the client: ordinary consciousness, mindful consciousness, riding the rapids, and the child stage. Therapy is not linear but goes in and out of each of these phases.

Indicators/Measures of Success

This process takes its cues from the pace of the child. It sometimes takes time for the child to let go of suspicions about the therapist's agenda and feel trusting and secure. This is a painstaking process and does not yield quick results. The "transformation" may take years.

Suggested Readings and Resources

http://nas.com/~richf/hakomi.htm

Johanson, G., and C. Taylor. "Hakomi Therapy with Seriously Emotionally Disturbed Adolescents." In Charles Schaefer, ed. *Innovative Interventions in Child and Adolescent Therapy* (New York: John Wiley & Sons, 1988).

Horticulture Therapy

When to Use the Technique

Although horticulture therapy is currently popular for physically challenged and geriatric populations, it is used with children who have self-esteem problems and other problems that can benefit from the child being put in a caregiving role. This technique lends itself to groups.

Patient Age and Profile

No specific age guidelines are available for horticulture therapy. Children can learn nurturing and social skills, problem-solving, and patience through this technique in conjunction with other interventions. Children with multiple problems, including physical limitations, can also benefit from this approach.

How the Technique Works

Many aspects of gardening can be utilized therapeutically. Preparing the soil can be physically demanding, allowing the child to vent and safely channel feelings of aggression and anger. Planting seeds and seedlings is an optimistic act of hope and planning. Tending a garden requires nurturing and responsibility. The context is interactive, purposeful, and productive. Plants provide a model that allows some distancing for the therapist and child to discuss relevant themes in growth, development, and needs.

Indicators/Measures of Success

Measures of success depend on the specific therapeutic goals intended. For example, is the child less depressed? Has he or she taken a less passive and more active role in relationships?

Suggested Readings and Resources

American Horticultural Therapy Association: www.ahta.org

Definition

Horticulture therapy uses processes in nature, specifically the sowing of seeds and the nurturing and growth of plants, to promote healing and healthy development in children. This technique was used by Friends Hospital in Philadelphia in 1879 when its parent institution built the first greenhouse for the purpose of therapeutic mental health.

Technique

Ignoring

Definition

Ignoring is a technique used mostly by parents and teachers to help set limits for young children and redirect their behavior toward more desirable activities.

When to Use the Technique

This technique is used under a fairly limited set of circumstances:

- when the undesirable behavior is relatively minor, harmless, and annoying;

- after the caregiver has already explained the technique at a prior time to the child;

- when the caregiver is about to lose control. This technique can "buy time" for the adult to cool down.

Patient Age and Profile

The child must be old enough to be able to understand the intent and consequence of this technique for it to serve as a useful aversive intervention.

How the Technique Works

Ignoring merely involves the withdrawal of attention by the parent or caregiver when the child engages in inappropriate, but not dangerous, behavior and the resumption of contact when the child returns to appropriate behavior. Ignoring means promptly and totally disengaging from the child while he or she is misbehaving; this means turning away and providing no verbal, eye, or body contact (Kernberg and Chazan, 1991).

It is important to use this technique in coordination with positive attention when the child behaves in desirable ways, so that the child readily understands and associates the connections between actions and consequences. It should be used very selectively, because it is possible to lose track of what the child is doing and this could quickly escalate into a harmful situation.

Indicators/Measures of Success

If the child gets the message fairly promptly and ceases the inappropriate behavior, this indicates that the technique is effective.

Suggested Readings and Resources

Kernberg, Paulina, and Saralea Chazan. *Children with Conduct Disorders: A Psychotherapy Manual*. New York: Basic Books, 1991.

"It's Not My Fault" (INMF)

When to Use the Technique

This technique can be helpful for work with traumatized or abused children.

Patient Age and Profile

James (1989) asserts that children as young as four can understand the complexities involved in this process when the situation is made clear to them.

How the Technique Works

In this approach, a child who has been traumatized or abused is told strongly and unequivocally that the traumatizing event was not his or her fault, but that the child may not believe that for a while. The child's need to hold on to his or her beliefs and express them is supported, while the clinician gently, relentlessly, directly, indirectly, and subliminally teaches the child that he or she was not to blame. If the child has actually been blamed by others, the clinician should insist that the child is not at fault and that the blaming person was in error.

> ### Definition
>
> INMF is an approach that guides or underscores therapy with traumatized or abused children. From the outset, children are assured unequivocally that the incident or event was not their fault—unless they were, in fact, responsible.

Storytelling and puppet play are excellent ways to foster the INMF theory. A child can be asked to tell a story about a puppy who did something wrong. The owner later got hurt, and the puppy felt that it must have been at fault. Or, during puppet play, the therapist can set up a story such as this one, told to a patient by James:

The scene involves a little girl who was very sick. When the parents brought her to the doctor, he said she had diabetes, an illness that made her feel terrible whenever she ate anything with sugar in it, like candy and soda. The doctor told the parents they should be very careful and not let their daughter eat anything sweet. They questioned the doctor to make sure they really understood. A week later, when they went shopping, the dad let the girl have a candy bar. He knew it was wrong, but he did it anyway, and the girl got very sick.

James and the child acted out this scenario, and then James asked the child to answer the following:

• Who did the wrong thing?

• What if the little girl purposely didn't try to stop the father from buying the candy bar?

- What if she enjoyed the candy?

- What if she really wanted it?

- What if she begged for it?

The process teaches and reinforces the notion that a good person, or one you love, is capable of doing something wrong without having to be viewed as totally bad. This exercise can enable a child to feel okay about any affectionate feelings he or she may have toward an abusive parent.

James reports that some of her colleagues disagree with this approach, believing that the child should be allowed full expression first, before the therapist tells the child that it's not his or her fault, and that the therapist should remain neutral until that happens. But James maintains that, "it is essential to present the clear, emphatic, unequivocal view that the child is not responsible for the trauma unless it is true…"

Children love to yell out the window, with the therapist, "IT'S NOT MY FAULT!" Kids who will not say INMF, or who do so halfheartedly, will readily say the words when they can yell them out the window. "This is a powerful exercise," James writes. "Yelling freely to the general public seems to imprint the message and counteracts feelings of self-blame. The child first tells the universe and then learns to tell himself. It's like peeling an orange—one starts from the outside and moves inward."

Variations have included making posters with the child's picture above the initials *INMF,* INMF badges to wear at home, INMF prayers, and INMF dances.

Indicators/Measures of Success

Children need opportunities to validate their expression of feelings surrounding traumatic incidents. They must integrate conflicted feelings towards the person who has "wronged" them. When children are able to make sense of what has happened to them, to internalize the fact that what has happened is not their fault, and to master their feelings of anxiety, guilt, and helplessness, this approach will have served its purpose.

Suggested Readings and Resources

James, Beverly. *Treating Traumatized Children: New Insights and Creative Interventions.* New York: Free Press, 1989.

Life Books

When to Use the Technique

The Life book is a useful tool for children who have been separated from their families through foster care or adoption.

Patient Age and Profile

Children who are old enough to record their own experiences can create Life books.

How the Technique Works

As children move through the foster care system and into adoption, large portions of personal history are lost. They may not know who they have lived with, what their family background is, whether they have brothers or sisters, why their parents placed them, or even their original names. When used by children in placement, Life books contain stories and factual accounts dictated or written by the child as well as the child's own drawings. The use of time lines helps the child depict significant events of each year of his or her life, clarifying various moves and the significant people at each location.

Though the therapist must gather information in a direct, specific manner, Harrison (1988) warns that the professional must present the information with sensitivity and compassion, in as positive a light as possible, and in a way that will not further damage the child's self-image. Specific issues to include are:

- why the birth parents placed the child in foster care or up for adoption;

- information on every place that the child has lived, how long he or she was there (with specific dates), who the foster parents were, and why the child was moved;

- information about where the child's siblings are and whether they are with a stable family that is taking care of them;

- the court's role in the child's life (is it one of protection and not punishment?), why the child has a social worker, and what that person does.

> **Definition**
>
> Life books are documents created by individuals to record their life stories. Their purpose is to help people understand their own unique history and to simultaneously provide an opportunity for validation and release of feelings connected to any powerful memories. The information in a Life book is important to identity formation and general life adjustment.

- fears and expectations about leaving a foster home and going to another home, or returning to the parent's home;

- fears and feelings about how an adoption might affect the child, as well as wishes and expectations for his or her new environment.

Life books done with the help of the foster or adoptive parents can aid in bonding and assist in the attachment process.

The Life book is therapeutic in that it explains what has happened, helping children accept their situations. Not having a Life book may result in children with "confused realities whose fantasies and conflicts keep them from adjusting adequately to family life" (Harrison, 1988).

Indicators/Measures of Success

Aust (1981) states, "Growth in most of the children completing a Life Book has been shown in the child's having a more positive self-concept; a more realistic and accepting view of self, parents and environment; a better understanding of where he has been and where he is going; improved memory; more appropriate social behavior; an increase in academic skills; a more realistic 'cover story' for his situation, rather than one involving fantasy or self-blame; improved interpersonal relationships; and increased tolerance of separation and change."

Suggested Readings and Resources

Aust, P. "Using the Life Story Book to Treat Children in Placement." *Child Welfare,* 60: 535-560.

Harrison, JoAnn. "Making Life Books with Foster and Adoptive Children." In C. Schaefer, ed. *Innovative Interventions in Child and Adolescent Therapy* (New York: John Wiley & Sons, 1988).

Mediation

When to Use the Technique

This process, a less adversarial alternative to litigation, is recommended with children involved in custody situations as a result of their parents' divorce. It is most often used in making decisions about with whom the children will live.

Patient Age and Profile

Children of all ages who are involved in custody disputes can benefit from this process.

How the Technique Works

Mediation as a problem-solving process focuses on (1) the needs and interests of the participants, (2) achieving fairness, (3) insuring privacy, (4) providing self-determination, and (5) discovering the best interests of all family members. In mediation, the decision making rests with both parties. The mediator is present to reduce obstacles to communication, maximize the exploration of alternatives, and address the needs of all involved.

Children are often a part of the mediation process. Everett and Volgy (1989) suggest that there are four main reasons to include them:

- to allow children to talk with a neutral party about their fears and concerns regarding their parents' divorce;

- to allow the mediator to evaluate each child's developmental level and needs so as to help the parents make informed decisions about living arrangements;

- to help defuse parental disputes and unrealistic demands, clearing the way for appropriate and flexible solutions; and

- to provide support for the parents when they reveal the outcome of the custody decision to their children.

This approach has several benefits. First, it protects the children by providing for a less chaotic environment, by encouraging rapid resumption of parenting functions by both parents, and by helping the parents to recognize that their conflicts may be secondary to the goal of

> ### Definition
>
> Mediation is a family-oriented conflict resolution process that is often used in child custody cases. An impartial third party usually assists the participants in negotiating a settlement.

taking care of the children. It also recognizes that possession of the children is an emotionally charged issue for parents.

Indicators/Measures of Success

If parents can be helped to work through their emotions and to end up feeling that they are still good parents, the technique can be considered successful; this outcome can also set the stage for better cooperation down the road.

Suggested Readings and Resources

Everett, C., and S. Volgy. "Mediating Child Custody Disputes." In M. Textor, ed. *The Divorce and Divorce Therapy Handbook* (Northvale, N.J.: Jason Aronson, 1989).

Friedman, Gary. *A Guide to Divorce Mediation.* New York: Workman Press, 1993.

Gardner, Richard A. *Family Evaluation in Child Custody: Mediation, Arbitration, and Litigation.* Cresskill, N.J.: Creative Therapeutics, 1989.

Meditation

When to Use the Technique

Meditation can help anxious, upset, or distracted children gain better control over their responses to stress. It can benefit youngsters who need a "retreat for refurbishing," whose alarm level is inappropriately high, or who need a nonmedical, "natural" tranquilizer (Carrington, 1982). Meditation is often used as part of a larger program of relaxation training.

Patient Age and Profile

Fish (1988) notes that a readiness pretest can be used to determine whether a young child or one who has developmental disabilities can sit still and follow instructions well enough to learn how to meditate. However, since practice is important in developing this technique, motivation is also a factor.

How the Technique Works

Meditation is an ancient human tool and there are many models for it, including Zen, yoga, and transcendental meditation. Most approaches have certain elements in common. The meditator should:

- find a quiet place;

- get comfortable, but not lie down and go to sleep;

- focus attention on a single thing—an object or a particular word, perhaps one given to him or her by the therapist;

- adopt a temporary 'let it go' attitude;

- practice the process for ten to twenty minutes twice a day.

Indicators/Measures of Success

Studies show that a meditative state is different, both physically and mentally, from the typical conscious state and also different from sleep. Differences in alpha brain waves and oxygen consumption have been measured. But it is the impact of meditation over time on the functioning of the child that interests therapists the most. Is the child less symptomatic? Does he or she have less anxiety? More energy? Is the

Definition

Meditation is a relaxation process aimed at achieving inner calm, which can then support a child in coping with his or her external environment.

child more efficacious? Does the child function more confidently in school and social settings? Is the child's behavior more appropriate?

If the answers to these questions are yes, the technique can be judged successful.

Suggested Readings and Resources

Benson, Herbert. *The Relaxation Response.* New York: William Morrow and Company, 1975.

Carrington, Patricia. "Meditation Techniques in Clinical Practice." In Lawrence Abt and Irving Stuart, ed. *The Newer Therapies: A Sourcebook* (New York: Van Nostrand Reinhold Company, 1982).

Fish, Marian. "Relaxation Training for Childhood Disorders." In Charles Schaefer, ed. *Innovative Interventions in Child and Adolescent Therapy* (New York: John Wiley & Sons, 1988).

Modeling

When to Use the Technique

Modeling—also called observational learning (Kazdin, 1985)—is often used with children who lack certain social skills, who are particularly shy, or who are aggressive. It has been used with youngsters who are afraid to speak in a group, with autistic children, and with those who exhibit deviant behaviors.

Patient Age and Profile

Imitation is a skill possessed even by the youngest children. Research on modeling as a specific therapy includes youngsters between the ages of five and seven, as well as adolescents and older teens. The therapy can address a range of problems, from anxiety disorders to violent behavior.

How the Technique Works

The technique is based on the power of learning from example; youngsters learn what they see. Modeling takes many different forms, depending on the circumstances involved. In some cases, modeling involves watching an admired peer execute a task that the child might find intimidating, and then trying to duplicate it. Occasionally, the therapist models the appropriate behavior. In some cases, the therapist encourages group role playing to practice the desired behaviors.

Videos and feedback discussions are often built into the process. Depending on the child's level of sophistication and the type of behavior being modeled, the therapist might ask the child to keep a log or to take notes on specific aspects of the model behavior. Positive feedback, usually social approval or affirmation but sometimes more concrete rewards, may serve to reinforce the modeling.

Strayhorn (1994) offers stories, plays, songs, and dances to support parents in modeling constructive activities for and with their children. Even as background tapes, these devices can put preferred role models and language into the child's memory bank for later use.

Definition

Modeling is the process of learning new behavioral repertoires by observing those behaviors in others. Although it is possible to learn undesirable behaviors by imitation, this intervention emphasizes using only positive examples worthy of emulation.

Indicators/Measures of Success

Successful replication of the desired behavior is one clear objective. Progress is also indicated if the child is able to continue implementing the model behavior even after he or she is weaned from external reinforcements. One looks specifically for reductions in the frequency or intensity of undesirable behaviors; genuine emotional responses or reduced anxiety reflects progress.

Suggested Readings and Resources

Kazdin, Alan. *Treatment of Antisocial Behavior in Children and Adolescents*. Homewood, Illinois: The Dorsey Press, 1985.

Strayhorn, Joseph. "Psychological Competence-Based Therapy for Young Children and Their Parents." In Craig LeCroy, ed. *Handbook of Child and Adolescent Treatment Manuals* (New York Lexington Books, 1994).

Thompson, Charles, and Linda Rudolph. *Counseling Children*. Pacific Grove, CA: Brooks Cole Publishing Company, 1996.

Van Hasselt, Vincent, D. Griest, A. Kazdin, K. Esvelt-Dawson, and A. Unis. "Treating Poor Peer Interactions on a Psychiatric Inpatient Unit." In Charles Schaefer, Howard Millman, Steven Sichel, and Jane Zwilling, eds. *Advances in Therapies for Children* (San Francisco: Jossey-Bass Publishers, 1986).

The Music Lesson

When to Use the Technique

This approach is thought to help increase a child's tolerance for new and unexpected sounds, a capability that can be generalized to many behavioral contexts. It can be used for youngsters who are aggressive and rebellious, school phobic, sensory-deprived, withdrawn, or anxious.

Patient Age and Profile

This is an age-flexible technique. It is considered valuable in many contexts, including group and individual therapy.

How the Technique Works

Ostwald (1968) believes that all feelings can be re-experienced in the context of the Music Lesson, which serves as a metaphor to prepare a child for all performances in life. The actual lessons teach a youngster "reverence for the equipment," which, in most instances, includes the child's own body. They also include athletic elements and learning breathing and tension/relaxation techniques. In combining action and symbols, the child feels intense emotions and learns a meaningful way to express them. Musical power can be used to both stimulate and soothe, and the child can learn to harness that power. Music incorporates mathematics and order, areas that older children can master and transfer to academic disciplines. Music contains what Ostwald calls "organized silence." Its study can help a child understand and appreciate silence and communication.

Indicators/Measures of Success

Musical proficiency is not the primary goal of the therapeutic Music Lesson, though this can be an outcome. Instead, the therapist looks for enhanced confidence, empathy, focus, control, and other changes that the technique was utilized to foster.

Suggested Readings and Resources

Ostwald, Peter. "The Music Lesson." In E. Thayer Gaston, ed. *Music In Therapy* (New York: Macmillan, 1968).

Definition

The Music Lesson is an adjunct therapy that can provide children with a range of therapeutic benefits, from developing improved concentration to release and relaxation of tension. It also helps satisfy the basic human need of being listened to (Ostwald, 1968).

Technique

Music With "Mum"

Definition

Music with "Mum" is a technique popularized by Margaret Shephard in Oxfordshire, England, to promote mother-child bonding (McMahon, 1992).

It uses action songs to connect young children with their primary caregiver. Music is used in similar ways in other contexts to facilitate communication and build relationships between a child and a caring adult.

When to Use the Technique

When attachment is weak or has been disrupted, this technique can prove productive. Mothers who have parenting or bonding skill deficits can use this tool to learn while simultaneously serving their child's needs. It is often used with nonverbal and autistic children.

Patient Age and Profile

Shephard's groups target babies and mothers, toddlers and mothers, and children under five with mothers. Children with learning deficits of all ages can benefit from music interactions.

How the Technique Works

Musical games that emphasize eye-body contact are selected. Lap games, knee-bouncing, and activity songs involve the mother-child pairs in playful, supportive functions. These activities are encouraged at home to strengthen the new patterns of relationship.

In situations where an older child is nonverbal, music can be used to "initiate conversations" and "tune in" to the child (McMahon). Here the therapist, parent, or educator follows the child and reflects in spontaneous song the activity in which the child is engaging. The song is designed to create a sort of dialogue by validating and expressing what the child is doing.

Indicators/Measures of Success

Signs of a strengthening of the relationship, both inside and outside of the therapeutic setting, indicate the effectiveness of this tool.

Suggested Readings and Resources

McMahon, Linnet. *The Handbook of Play Therapy.* London: Routledge, 1992.

My Inner Critic

When to Use the Technique

Originally designed for abused children, this technique may also be helpful for use with those who are experiencing behavioral difficulties.

Patient Age and Profile

Children aged seven through twelve can benefit from this technique.

How the Technique Works

To begin, children should be told that everyone has an "inner critic" that says mean or critical things. Examples include, "Paul, you're too fat," when Paul looks in the mirror, or "Sue, you're a dope," when Sue gets an answer wrong. Therapists should use themselves as examples. Children should make lists of the mean things their inner critics say to them and then compare their lists. Pearce and Pezzot-Pearce (1997) suggest that children with behavioral difficulties such as physical aggression may be encouraged to identify the negative self-statements associated with these problems (e.g., "I'm a bad kid, and everyone hates me because I torment the other kids").

When the children become aware of making these covert self-statements, they can learn to make the critic stop. They are instructed to visualize a stop sign, and every time the inner critic starts to say something negative, they are taught to say "Stop!" to themselves and immediately replace the negative statement with a more positive one (e.g., "I made a mistake, but I'm learning to control my temper," or "I'm still okay, even if some of the things I do are not okay").

The therapist may have to prompt the child to use this strategy or to provide tangible reminders of the child's strengths when he or she becomes especially anxious. These strengths should be incorporated into self-statements that the child should use whenever he or she feels threatened by explorations and discussions of the problem behavior.

Pearce and Pezzot-Pearce assert that children need repeated practice to learn to implement this technique. The therapist can help children practice changing their negative thoughts into positive ones by

Definition

In this strategy, children are asked to identify and then extinguish their negative self-statements.

presenting a variety of self-statements, including those associated with problem behaviors. The children are then asked to replace these negative thoughts with positive ones. For children who remain reluctant to acknowledge their behavior directly, the therapist may present a more detailed scenario that involves a child who also does not want to talk about embarrassing or shameful behavior. This scenario introduces sensitive material somewhat indirectly by recounting a hypothetical child's behavior, and then by asking the patient to identify some of the negative thoughts of this child, as well as the positive thoughts that might replace them.

Indicators/Measures of Success

Therapy to change the cognitive distortions of abuse-reactive children is successful when children are able to demonstrate the use of positive self-statements to cope with negative feelings and actions. Their self-esteem will increase, and they will feel more confident, competent, cherished by some, and worthwhile to others.

Suggested Readings and Resources

Cunningham, Carol, and Kee Macfarlane. *When Children Abuse: Group Treatment Strategies for Children with Impulse Control Problems.* Brandon, VT: Safer Society Press, 1991.

Pearce, James, and Terry Pezzot-Pearce. *Psychotherapy with Abused and Neglected Children.* New York: The Guilford Press, 1997.

Negative Practice

When to Use the Technique

Negative practice is not considered as strong a technique for habit elimination as competing response training (see competing response training on pp. 31 to 32]. However, it is still applied to nervous behaviors such as tics and stuttering and to aggressive behaviors such as fire setting.

Patient Age and Profile

Patients as young as six years old have shown improvements by using this technique.

How the Technique Works

The undesirable behavior that is targeted for elimination is prescribed on a daily routine. Depending on the problem, the unwanted behavior can be practiced for a fixed amount of time following each occurrence, or it could be practiced in a standardized way under (usually parental) supervision. In the case of fire setting, the behavior is set up in a controlled setting and followed by a corrective/clean-up regimen. With a tic, the child is expected to engage in tic practice every day for approximately thirty minutes. Reinforcement is sometimes provided.

The reasoning behind this technique is speculative. Some hypotheses are that negative practice increases voluntary control over the behavior, that it desensitizes the child to the issues around the behavior, and that it reflects paradoxical intention.

Indicators/Measures of Success

The best indication of success is the continued reduction of the problem behavior.

Suggested Readings and Resources

Kolko, David. "Multicomponent Parental Treatment of Firesetting in a Six-Year-Old Boy." *Journal of Behavior Therapy and Experimental Psychiatry*, 14(4): 349-353. In Charles Schaefer, Howard Millman, Steven Sichel, and Jane Zwilling, eds. *Advances in Therapies for Children* (San Francisco: Jossey-Bass, 1986).

Schroeder, Carolyn, and Betty Gordon. *Assessment and Treatment of Childhood Problems: A Clinician's Guide.* New York: The Guilford Press, 1991.

Definition

Negative practice, sometimes referred to as contingent negative practice, is a technique for eliminating unwanted behavior by indulging in it. The idea is to engage in the behavior with the cooperation of others rather than to fight it.

Technique

Overlearning

When to Use the Technique

Overlearning is practiced after some skills have already been developed. It can be used to reduce the likelihood of relapse.

Patient Age and Profile

This process is used on the same children who use the urine alarm training, between the ages of approximately five and thirteen.

How the Technique Works

Overlearning can begin in the middle of the urine alarm training, after the youngster has developed greater awareness and control of his or her bladder pressure. One rule of thumb for when to start overlearning is after the child has accomplished seven consecutive dry nights. He or she is expected to consume extra large amounts of water before retiring at night (Schaefer [1997] suggests two pints). This places an extra physical burden on the training but presumably enhances the probability that the results will be more enduring.

In overlearning, it is also recommended that the youngster remain with the training until he or she has accomplished double the number of dry consecutive nights proposed in the original training (bringing the recommended number to fourteen, allowing for one accident).

Indicators/Measures of Success

Continued success in maintaining dry nights is a critical measure of success of this technique.

Suggested Readings and Resources

Schaefer, Charles. *Childhood Encopresis and Enuresis: Causes and Therapy.* Northvale, N.J.: Jason Aronson, 1997.

Taylor, Peter, and R. Keith Turner. "A Clinical Trial of Continuous, Intermittent and Overlearning 'Bell and Pad' Treatments for Nocturnal Enuresis." *Behaviour Research and Therapy,* 13: 281-293. In Charles Schaefer and Howard Millman. *Therapies for Children* (San Francisco: Jossey-Bass, 1977).

Definition

Overlearning is a technique often used in conjunction with the urine alarm/bell-and-pad treatment to stop bedwetting. Overlearning starts with the progress already accomplished in the training and stretches its limits in an effort to solidify and strengthen these gains.

Pair Painting

When to Use the Technique

Teachers and other group leaders can use this activity when children need a "boost" in their sharing and cooperating skills.

Patient Age and Profile

Young children can best appreciate this technique, but older children who are open to new experiences can benefit from it as well.

How the Technique Works

In this technique, which was actually created by two young students who had to share an easel, pairs of children using one easel take turns brushing paint onto a large piece of paper, adding onto each other's lines and strokes. Each time one adds a stroke, he or she chants, "Now this goes on yours." This process is repeated over and over, back and forth. As they paint, the pace is speeded up, as are the chants. Variations in activities and chants include:

- focusing on color ("Now I'm putting black on yours," "Now I'm putting yellow on yours");

- specific kinds of brush strokes ("Now here goes a dot," "Now here goes a circle");

- back-and-forth chants sung to familiar tunes; and

- efforts to represent real objects ("Now here goes an eye on the face," "Now here goes a mouth on the face").

Children can share their paintings at class meetings, and they should be encouraged to talk about how they made them, to describe how they worked together, and to recite the chants they made up. By sharing their painting techniques, they give each other new things to try and see that they together generate new ideas. Variations of pair painting include pair block building and alternating putting objects away at cleanup time.

Indicators/Measures of Success

If this class activity matches the abilities and interests of young children, it should promote cooperation and fun rather than competition.

Definition

Pair painting involves two children creating a painting together, each taking turns making brush strokes. It is just one of a variety of cooperative activities that foster a give-and-take relationship between children in a classroom environment.

Working together can help children learn to take into account each other's point of view when deciding how to act, and it can give them the satisfaction of contributing and accomplishing something tangible when working with others.

Levin (1994) writes, "While the teacher could never have predicted where the pair paintings would lead, it became a central theme or ritual for organizing the social interactions and curriculum in that...classroom. As the children played their pair games, they were also developing language and representational skills, as well as such concepts as logical causality, reciprocity, and color mixing."

Suggested Readings and Resources

Levin, Diane. *Teaching Young Children in Violent Times.* Cambridge, MA: Educators for Social Responsibility, 1994.

Paradoxical Procedure: A Bet with the Patient

When to Use the Technique

Instead of opposing families who cling to their problem behaviors, therapists can use paradoxical techniques to ally with them. Situations where children have resisted change, where they are caught in a larger network into which the problem behavior feeds, and where they tend to oppose the therapist are appropriate contexts for this approach. The paradoxical bet is also often successfully used in school settings.

Patient Age and Profile

Adolescents are particularly good candidates for paradoxical interventions such as "The Bet" because they tend to be oppositional in their attempt to achieve independence. Low motivation and difficulty in life-cycle transitions also characterize the children for whom this technique is recommended (Sherman and Fredman, 1986).

How the Technique Works

Offering a bet to the child concerning his or her behavior is a technique that acknowledges some value or useful role for the problem behavior, while paradoxically calling upon it to effect therapeutic change. The therapist explains or predicts how the problem behavior serves the child and then bets the youngster that he or she cannot stop the behavior. The bet hinges on the adolescent's desire to defy the therapist and the prediction. In order to win the bet, the youngster will either improve or cease the problem behavior. The child wins when he or she controls the problem.

One example cited by Sherman and Fredman (1986) concerned students who were sent out of a seventh-grade classroom for fighting (Williams and Weeks, 1984). The boys pleaded innocence to the administrator, claiming instead that the teacher had overreacted. The administrator made an implicit bet with the children that if they acted the same way in their next class, the second teacher would react the same way. The boys were directed to continue to fight as they had in the first class to allow the administrator to check out the unfairness of the first teacher. If subsequent teachers sent them out of class again, however, this would

Definition

In paradoxical procedures, the therapist takes advantage of the child's chronic or rigid adherence to the problem behavior, using resistance to authority (or contradictions in the system created by that behavior) in order to clarify the dynamics of the problem and motivate change in behavior. The paradoxical bet is constructed so that the child will win the bet against the therapist or counselor when he or she alters the behavior in a constructive way.

indicate that the boys were indeed misbehaving, and punishment would be appropriate. The boys won the bet by correcting their behavior and remaining in class.

Indicators/Measures of Success

Success is evidenced by a change in the problem behavior. However, it is conceivable—though unlikely—that the problem behavior could persist, resulting in the therapist winning the bet. In such a case, the youngster's actions would confirm the version of the problem expressed by the therapist. Under these circumstances, at least, the dynamics behind the child's behavior would be exposed and overt and the child confronted with a clear choice.

Suggested Readings and Resources

McMullin, Rian. *Handbook of Cognitive Therapy Techniques.* New York: W.W. Norton and Company, 1986.

Papp, Peggy. "Treatment of a Child's Underachievement in School Using a Paradoxical Approach with the Family." In Charles Schaefer, James Briesmeister, and M. Fitton, eds. *Family Therapy Techniques for Problem Behaviors of Children and Teenagers* (San Francisco: Jossey-Bass Publishers, 1984).

Sherman, Robert, and Norman Fredman. *Handbook of Structured Techniques in Marriage and Family Therapy.* New York: Brunner/Mazel, Publishers, 1986.

Williams, J., and Gerald Weeks. "Use of Paradoxical Techniques in a School Setting." *American Journal of Family Therapy,* 12(3): 47-56.

Paraverbal Therapy

When to Use the Technique

Heimlich (1981) used this technique with depressed, acting-out children. McDonnell (1979) exposed it with traumatically injured and chronically ill children to reduce their emotional disturbance. The technique has also been utilized with selectively mute and conduct-disordered children.

Patient Age and Profile

Children ages four through twelve can benefit from this technique.

How the Technique Works

Paraverbal therapy creates a pleasurable, stimulating, and reciprocal interaction between the child and therapist. Its goal is to reduce stresses by providing an experience of human closeness and shared pleasure, with opportunities for motor release (McDonnell).

In one example offered by Heimlich, a drum was used as a simple percussive medium to engage the child in individual tapping, in rhythmic dialogue with the therapist, or in synchronous performance. This provided a base for communication, a feeling of pleasure and competence, and the discharge of tension.

McDonnell improvised a song on an autoharp at the bedside of a severely burned four-year-old boy and allowed him to use the instrument and any others he asked for. During ten paraverbal therapy sessions, the boy was given many choices as to instruments and song lyrics. McDonnell encouraged the boy to express his thoughts and feelings about painful hospital procedures, his accident, and his feelings of homesickness.

As confidence and trust develop, the instruments can be used to communicate a specific affect. For example, cymbals can be struck together loudly and quickly to convey anger, or softly and slowly to convey sadness. Heimlich comments, "A different sound-dominated maneuver employs the voice, which can be used with or without words… In paraverbal therapy, the media are used solely for

Definition

This multisensory "expressive media" technique employs a variety of maneuvers to achieve nonverbal communication in addition to ordinary speech. "Maneuvers" refer to the ways the nonverbal communications, in the form of sounds or movements, are used.

communication and treatment, not for formal learning or esthetic purposes, although these are often by-products" (p. 263).

Heimlich has used paraverbal therapy to treat two children at once. For example, an aggressive child who needed to develop "people skills" as well as appropriate communicative behavior became an "assistant therapist," using paraverbal therapy with a depressed, selectively mute child. At the end of ten sessions, the first child's acting-out behavior was resolved, and the selectively mute child talked more to peers and adults.

Indicators/Measures of Success

"As a tool for lessening emotional distress, this technique can quickly focus on central areas of anxiety and concern for the patients," McDonnell maintains. "Paraverbal therapy can allow the appropriate discharge of tensions as well as communication of painful feelings." In her treatment of the burned boy, his spontaneous comments and his responses to questions about a song's content led to discussions that enabled him to relive the specific trauma of the accident and to tolerate the fears, pain, and loneliness attendant to being in the hospital.

Suggested Readings and Resources

Heimlich, Evelyn. "Patient as Assistant Therapist in Paraverbal Therapy with Children." *American Journal of Psychotherapy,* 35: 262-267.

McDonnell, L. "Paraverbal Therapy in Pediatric Cases with Emotional Complications." *American Journal of Orthopsychiatry,* 19(1): 44-52.

Schaefer, Charles, Howard Millman, Steven Sichel, and Jane Zwilling, eds. *Advances in Therapies for Children* (San Francisco: Jossey-Bass, 1986)

Parent-Child Interaction Therapy

When to Use the Technique

This technique works best with children who are displaying such behaviors as noncompliance, aggression, overactivity, destructiveness, or temper tantrums.

Patient Age and Profile

Children between the ages of two and five are the best subjects for this intervention.

How the Technique Works

PCIT's basic premise is that parents have enormous influence over their young children's behavioral and emotional development, and that some of these influences may cause or exacerbate problems. Just as parents may negatively influence their children's behavior, so too do they have enormous power to influence their young children in a therapeutic way. PCIT takes full advantage of this principle and recognizes that the power a therapist has to influence a young child pales in comparison to the power parents have to produce change.

Through this intervention, behavioral problems are alleviated before they become ingrained. Research indicates that if these problems are "caught" early enough, the prognosis is very favorable for being able to reverse the behavioral patterns. Unfortunately, it has been widely believed that problems that occur during the preschool years will be "outgrown" as the child matures and develops. This is generally true for children whose behavior and developmental problems fall within normal limits of individual variability. But recent research has shown that many children do not outgrow these behaviors, and that they are at risk for adjustment problems in elementary school and beyond. If untreated, their problems can interfere with their development of self-help, socialization, and academic skills.

Throughout the therapy session, the therapist is behind a one-way mirror coaching the parent, who is wearing a hearing aid. The parent feels that he or she is the "therapist." By the therapist's helping the parent to learn specialized parenting skills, the child's behavior improves. For

Definition

Parent-child interaction therapy (PCIT) provides a basic framework for treating many of the problems that arise in childhood and directly involves the child's parents or caregivers in the therapy. The focus is on the destructive behaviors that seem to be intensified by the interaction patterns between parent and child.

example, the parent may say something to the child and immediately get feedback from the therapist. If he or she is having difficulty with the skill, the therapist will indicate something positive to do instead, such as, "Just turn and ignore that," or "Say 'I like it when you draw on the paper.'" Parents are told what to do rather than what they're doing wrong.

There are two stages involved in PCIT. In the first stage, which is called the relationship enhancement stage, a "warm and loving" relationship is established. It is designed to teach parents positive parenting skills. Parents are taught how to use active listening skills by learning to listen to their children and to communicate in a positive way. They are also taught to recognize their children's positive traits and to use ample praise to help the child's self-esteem problems. A very important skill is ignoring minor misbehaviors. Because these children engage in very high rates of misbehaviors, it is important that parents prioritize and learn that some of the misbehaviors are going to have to be ignored.

The second stage, which involves discipline, will not be effective unless a warm and positive nurturing relationship between parent and child has been established. This stage teaches parents to give effective directions to their child, and to provide consistent consequences for his or her misbehavior. Among other skills, parents are taught the "Do" and "Don't" skills in which they are asked to remember the acronym "D-R-I-P," which represents the first letter of each of the "do" skills (Describe, Reflect, Imitate, and Praise). Describing and Reflecting are largely active listening skills, Imitating helps the parent to get to the child's level, and Praise is the most important feedback for raising the child's self-esteem. Children with severe behavioral problems are at very high risk for low self-esteem.

For example, in the first discipline session, children are set up for success by doing "minding," which includes heeding exercises. Toys are put out on a table, and the parent (with the therapist's coaching) will say, "We're going to practice minding today. I'll give you lots of little instructions, like 'Please put the card in my hand,' or 'Please put the block in the box,' and when I tell you to do something, you need to listen. If you listen, I'll be very excited and very happy with you, and we'll be able to keep playing, and we can play what you want to play. If you don't listen, then you'll have to go to time-out." The child role plays the time-out procedure in advance and is given stickers for practicing.

The consequences for leaving time-out are also rehearsed and role-played with the child. When the child "minds," he or she is rewarded with a very enthusiastic statement. When the child does not mind, he or she is given a "two choices" statement, such as, "You have two choices. You can either put the block in the box or go to time-out." The process begins with instructions that are very simple and can be learned very quickly, and the children get lots of positive experience with minding. It actually becomes something that they enjoy doing. Once the minding rates are up, more and more difficult instructions that have to do with real life are given, such as picking up toys, coming inside, or taking the parent's hand for a walk. It is usually at these times that the child is more likely to become defiant. But he or she is now set up for success by having practiced listening, by having the idea that he or she is good at listening, and by thinking that everyone is proud of him or her for that.

Indicators/Measures of Success

PCIT expert Cheryl Bodiford-McNeil comments:

Children come in with many different behavior problems. They're whining, hitting, cursing. This program is unique in that we are not doing behavior modification for all of these separate behaviors. Instead we're targeting patterns. The two major patterns are associated with the two stages of the program. The first pattern and stage have to do with the negative attention-seeking behaviors, whining, noncompliance to serve the function of getting negative attention from their parents, which is very stimulating and very rewarding for these children.

The second pattern deals with the issue of noncompliance. These children have a basic disrespect for authority figures, and they don't want to listen when they're told to do something. The second part of the program works toward getting them to respect their parents and to comply when they're told to do so. We find that if we can get these kids to mind their parents, a lot of the other behavior problems are easier to deal with, and this paves the way to significant parent-child relationship improvements.

Suggested Readings and Resources

Braswell, Laura. "Involving Parents in Cognitive-Behavioral Therapy with Children and Adolescents. In Philip Kendall, ed. *Child and Adolescent Therapy*, 316-351 (New York: Guilford, 1991).

Hembree-Kigin, Toni, and Cheryl Bodiford McNeil. *Parent-Child Interaction Therapy*. New York: Plenum Press, 1995.

Technique

Parent Effectiveness Training (P.E.T.)

Definition

Parent Effectiveness Training (P.E.T.) refers to the principles and strategies formulated by Thomas Gordon, Ph.D. (1970) to provide parents with constructive alternatives to power struggles, escalating (but ineffective) punishment responses, and defiant and tuned-out scenarios with their children. P.E.T. offers a system of communication that is designed to enhance mutual respect and "no-lose" problem-solving within families.

When to Use the Technique

Gordon targets P.E.T. to society as a whole, because "parents are blamed, but not trained." He applies P.E.T. to families with children and teens and to those with children who have disabilities. He advocates using P.E.T. where "thousands of adolescents have fired their parents," as well as in a "preventative function" to prepare parents for effective and enjoyable parenthood. Gordon recommends the P.E.T. approach to help repair dysfunctional relationships and to eliminate rebellion and tantrums. It is particularly useful for addressing conflict within families.

Patient Age and Profile

Gordon (1970) claims that P.E.T. can work with parents in communicating with youngsters of all ages, including infants and toddlers. Parents model new attitudes and methods of communication, which are then adopted by other family members. Gordon says P.E.T. "can prevent war in the home, and bring parents and children closer rather than grouped against each other as hostile antagonists." Educators can also benefit from using P.E.T.

How the Technique Works

Parent Effectiveness Training claims to be "revolutionary" in rejecting power as the base for parental authority and rejecting punishment as a technique for coercing parental decisions. It teaches "how to listen so kids will talk to you" in order to help children express their own issues and emotions, and to promote accurate parent perspective and respect of the child's needs. The approach teaches parents how to distinguish between problems that belong to the parent, those that belong to the child, and those that belong to the relationship, so that responsibility for resolving the problem can be appropriately determined. Effective skill in using "active listening," "you-messages," and "I-messages" will enable parents "to talk so kids will listen."

P.E.T. assumes children are worthy of respect, capable of solving many problems, and can learn to be considerate and cooperative. It also assumes that since parents are not gods, they should interpret their parenting role as one of "helping agent."

The process relies on motivational research concerning resentment and resistance to revise "win-lose" relationships and instead foster dynamics geared to "no-lose" solutions. In "no-lose" situations, nobody is forced to submit to unacceptable choices, and participants' needs are heard and incorporated into a mutual agreement. Gordon explains by analogy that children are not possessions but should be accorded acceptance as separate human beings in the same way that parents might treat guests or peers.

Gordon advises parents to "bite their tongues and open their ears" if they want to encourage dialogue on serious matters with their children. Instead of taking over the child's problem, parents need to keep their attitude flexible and return the ball to the child. Instead of moralizing, parents can use "door openers" such as: "This seems like something important to you, " or "Your ideas are worthy of being listened to."

Punishment and threats are the wrong approach, Gordon believes, because they set in motion negative responses such as resistance, resentment, and defiance. Instead, most problems can be resolved by mutual agreement that takes into account the needs of each party. Gordon provides an example about a child who refuses to wear her plaid raincoat to school. The effective parent says:

Well, we really have a conflict here. You don't want to wear your raincoat because it's plaid, but I sure don't want to pay a cleaning bill, and I will not feel comfortable with you getting a cold. Can you think of a solution that we both could accept? How could we solve this so we're both happy?

The child came up with another coat that would substitute, and the problem disappeared.

Another technique Gordon suggests to parents to help change unacceptable behavior of children is to modify aspects of the environment. Making certain that closet hooks are at the child's level, and providing a child with an alarm clock, for example, facilitate taking responsibility and reduce frustration.

Indicators/Measures of Success

When P.E.T. is successfully implemented, participants demonstrate greater commitment to each other, to communication, and to the solutions that their joint efforts have created. More creative solutions arise, less time is needed for enforcement activities, and greater understanding of children (their actual problems and needs) is reported. Less conflict is perceived.

P.E.T. methods can backfire, however, when techniques are employed in attempts to manipulate or mold children to predetermined outcomes. Without some philosophical change on the part of those utilizing P.E.T. strategies, progress in relationships is unlikely.

Suggested Readings and Resources

Gordon, Thomas. *P.E.T.: Parent Effectiveness Training.* New York: Peter H. Wyden, Inc., 1970.

Parent Training

When to Use the Technique

This intervention has been especially helpful with conduct-disordered children and their parents, although its benefits can extend to children with virtually any problem or disorder.

Patient Age and Profile

Children aged four through seventeen can benefit from this intervention.

How the Technique Works

The reasons for and advantages of parent training include:

- Parents are with the child more than most other adult figures, and they have more power over the child than any other adult, including the clinician.

- Parents are often eager to learn and employ techniques, and they respond favorably when they are offered comprehensible and practical methods for becoming more competent.

- Parents do not merely stand in the background; they play an active part in the therapeutic endeavor and are directly and actively involved as co-therapists.

- Inviting parents to become "allies" in the therapeutic process gives them an enhanced sense of personal and parental competence.

- Partnership between the parents and clinician gives back dignity, respect, and self-control to parents who are often seeking help for their children's problems at a time when the parents are vulnerable to feelings of low self-esteem, guilt, and self-blame.

- Parent training is typically short-term (usually six to ten sessions) and is cost effective.

- Because parent training lends itself to group environments, it can be less expensive than individual therapy, and it offers the benefits of group dynamics as well.

Parent training groups consist optimally of a combination of six to eight individual parents or couples who typically meet once a week for two

---

Definition

Parent training uses parents as agents to treat children's problems or disorders. Training groups focus on parent behavior, as it is often assumed that the parent's behavior is responsible for the child's problem (i.e., a child's noncompliance is the result of the parent's commanding behavior). The aim is to change the behavior of the child by teaching parents to use more effective parenting techniques.

hours for ten weeks. The group cohesiveness that develops is an important element of the filial therapy process, and the interpersonal group support enhances parents' perception of themselves as being worthwhile and capable.

The parents and therapist sit in a circle and engage in discussion. Lengthy lectures are avoided. Training information is carefully introduced in connection with spontaneous parent concerns or information about their children. Solutions to problems and new ways to respond to children often originate within the group. Homework assignments are given at each session to help maintain involvement between sessions. Landreth's (1991) basic outline of each session is as follows:

Session 1. Parents get to know each other, describe their families, and characterize the child of focus. Goals and objectives of the training are explained. Homework involves identifying anger, happiness, sadness, and surprise in the child and making a reflective response.

Session 2. Homework assignments are reviewed, empathic (positive) responding is elaborated on, and the therapist demonstrates empathic responding with a volunteer, followed by the viewing of a videotape of the therapist in a play session with a child. Parents role-play in pairs in the playroom, taking turns being the parent and the child. Parents are given a list of toys and instructed to reserve these toys for playtime. The homework assignment is to put the toy "kit" together and to select a time and uninterrupted place in the home for the play sessions. Sessions may not be in the child's room, or interrupted for any reason.

Session 3. Parents report on arrangements they've made for their at-home play sessions. Play therapy skills are taught, including role-playing in the playroom, and a second videotape of the therapist in a play session with a child is viewed. Homework includes helping the child make a sign that reads "Play Session—Do Not Disturb" to hang on the door and to have the first play session. Parents adhere to the following rules:

DON'T:

- criticize any behavior;
- praise the child;
- ask leading questions;
- allow interruptions;
- offer information or teach;

- preach;

- initiate new activities; or

- be passive or quiet.

DO:

- set the stage;

- let the child lead;

- track behavior;

- reflect the child's feelings;

- set limits;

- salute the child's power and effort;

- join in the play as a follower; and

- be verbally active.

Cleanup is the responsibility of the parent; children can assist but may not continue to play after the time has ended. The parent must end the session even though the child might want to continue; thus the child learns that the parent can be firm and will follow through. Parents are reminded to make notes immediately following the session and to tell their child that they are going to a class to learn how to play with him or her. One parent volunteers to videotape a play session at home (or to be videotaped at the therapy center) and to bring the tape to the next session.

Session 4. Reports are given by each parent on the first session and areas of difficulty. Suggestions are offered by the therapist, and attention is given to the feelings the parents experienced. The videotape of the parent play session is viewed, and other parents give feedback. The therapist's goal is to find parental responses and behaviors in the videotape to support. Correction is kept to a minimum. Another parent volunteers to be videotaped.

Sessions 5-9. These sessions follow the same general format, including brief reporting on play sessions, viewing of videotape, and critiquing of homework. Training principles and role-playing skills are reviewed. Newly developed parental coping skills are identified to help parents feel a sense of personal power. Generalization of skills outside the sessions typically occurs at this time. Homework assignments can include having parents make three therapeutic limit-setting responses to typical happenings outside the play session.

Session 10. Parents report on their play sessions, a parent session is viewed, and the last hour is spent with parents sharing their evaluation of the experience and how they and the children have changed. Parents also share their perceptions of changes they have observed in other parents. The therapist shares notes of parents' original description of their children as points of reference to evaluate progress. For the most part, this is a very rewarding time for the whole group.

Indicators/Measures of Success

Parent training programs have resulted in positive changes that have been maintained for over four years after formal treatment. Techniques learned in parent training have been generalized to behaviors other than those initially targeted, and parents have proven to be capable of generalizing their newly acquired therapeutic skills to other children in the family.

Suggested Readings and Resources

Forehand, R., and Robert McMahon. *Helping the Noncompliant Child: A Clinician's Guide to Parent Training.* New York: The Guilford Press, 1981.

Landreth, Gary. *Play Therapy: The Art of the Relationship.* Muncie, IN: Accelerated Development Inc., 1991.

Schaefer, Charles, and J. Breismeister, eds. *Handbook of Parent Training: Parents as Co-Therapists for Children's Behavior Problems.* New York: John Wiley & Sons, 1989.

Webster-Stratton, Carolyn, and Martin Herbert. *Troubled Families, Problem Children.* New York: John Wiley & Sons, 1994.

Peer Initiation Training

When to Use the Technique

This technique was originally developed for use with children who were socially withdrawn but otherwise normal. It can be used, however, to remediate the social unrelatedness of autistic children as well.

Patient Age and Profile

Autistic children of elementary school age can be helped through this technique.

How the Technique Works

As used with autistic children, several preliminary sessions are devoted to training a peer to initiate toy play interactions. The teacher plays the role of an autistic child and uses instructions, modeling, and praise to teach the peer. For half of the trials, the teacher complies with the peer's toy play initiations; for the other half, the teacher ignores the initiations in order to prepare the child for behaviors likely to occur with the autistic child. The peer is taught to persist until the teacher finally complies. The content of peer initiation training typically involves some or all of the following elements:

1. **Organizing play.** The peer specifies an activity, suggests an idea for play, or directs another child to engage in a play behavior.

2. **Sharing.** The peer offers or gives an object to the other child or accepts an object from the other child.

3. **Making a request for sharing.** The peer asks the other child to give him or her an object.

4. **Assisting.** The peer helps the other child complete a task or desired action.

5. **Complimenting.** The peer uses verbal statements indicating praise, affection, or attraction.

6. **Showing affection.** The peer uses hugging, patting, kissing, or holding hands to demonstrate approval and liking.

Definition

This technique involves training normal children (peers) to initiate interactions with autistic and socially withdrawn children as a way of improving the existing social skills of the dysfunctional children.

Strain et al. (1979) advocate the use of this and other peer mediated interventions for a number of reasons. The first is that the use of peer mediators can extend social interventions to multiple children concurrently. A second reason derives from the findings that adult-mediated reinforcement may produce frequent but brief interactions that do not resemble natural, extended interactions in normal children. The third reason is that generalization and maintenance of social skills will more likely be the result if normal peers are actively involved in the intervention.

Indicators/Measures of Success

The initial extensions of this model to autistic children showed that the procedure was successful in rapidly bringing about increases in the social play of these children. For example, Ragland et al. (1978) taught a normal conduct-disordered boy to initiate toy play interactions with three autistic children. Each autistic child showed significant increases in social play with the peer confederate. However, in this and similar studies, little generalization of social interaction occurred in settings where the peer did not initiate interactions.

Suggested Readings and Resources

Newsom, Crighton, and Arnold Rincover. "Autism." In E. Mash and R. Barkley, eds. *Treatment of Childhood Disorders* (New York: The Guilford Press, 1989).

Ragland, E., M. Kerr, and P. Strain. "Behavior of Withdrawn Autistic Children: Effects of Peer Social Initiations." *Behavior Modification*, 2: 565-578.

Strain, P., M. Kerr, and E. Ragland. "Effects of Peer-Mediated Social Initiations and Prompting/Reinforcement Procedures in the Social Behavior of Autistic Children." *Journal of Autism and Developmental Disorders*, 9: 41-54.

Peer Pairing

When to Use the Technique

Children who demonstrate social phobias and avoidance of social situations can benefit from this technique.

Patient Age and Profile

Preschool and elementary age children are usually targeted with this intervention; however, it can be used with older children if they are amenable to it.

How the Technique Works

Beidel and Morris (1995) write, "Peer pairing treatment is conceptualized as the provision and structuring of a facilitative environment conducive to mutually reinforcing social interactional influences." Popular peers serve as ideal models of age-appropriate social behavior, and they provide social reinforcement for target children.

Furman et al. (1979) conducted a study in which children who engaged in peer interaction during less than 33 percent of the observations (and subsequently considered to be social isolates) were assigned to socially "normal" peers—some with younger partners, others with same-age partners, and still others to a control group. Each isolate and his or her partner participated in ten play sessions scheduled over a period of four to six weeks. During each session, the children played with two toys for approximately twenty minutes. Toys included blocks, puppets, felt and cardboard figures, dress-up clothing, and train sets.

The authors found that the play sessions with younger peers fostered increased peer interaction, perhaps because they provided situations in which assertive behaviors met with a higher probability of success than in the classroom. They concluded that "experiences with younger children, as contrasted with experiences with age mates, would provide the isolate with the most opportunities to initiate and direct social activity." (p. 921)

> ### Definition
>
> In peer pairing, a peer-mediated procedure, target children are provided opportunities to engage in activities with either "normal" or "popular status" peers to increase both positive social interaction and peer acceptance.

Indicators/Measures of Success

Changes in self-perceptions and cognitions following efficacy experiences with peers may alter the subsequent behavior of socially avoidant children (Beidel and Morris). Strain and Fox (1981) suggest that treatments incorporating a child's peers are often superior to adult-mediated approaches for remediating social isolation.

In the Furman study, social contact in a one-on-one situation with younger children was found to increase social activity of isolate children in their classrooms. Improvement among the isolate children who were exposed to younger children was so marked that post-treatment interaction was almost twice as frequent as pretreatment interaction—essentially at the same level as the social interaction of the nonisolate children. (p. 920)

Suggested Readings and Resources

Beidel, Deborah, and Tracy Morris. "Social Phobia." In J. March, ed. *Anxiety Disorders in Children and Adolescents* (New York: The Guilford Press, 1995).

Furman, Wyndol, Donald Rahe, and Willard Hartup. "Rehabilitation of Socially Withdrawn Preschool Children through Mixed-age and Same-age Socialization." *Child Development,* 50: 915-922.

Phototherapy

When to Use the Technique

The depression, fatigue, and carbohydrate cravings that accompany SAD are associated with relatively short daylight hours (in fall and winter in North America), and abate when day length increases (in spring). Estimates suggest that approximately 10 million people in the United States (about 6 percent of the population) suffer from SAD, with incidence highest in the northern states. It is not clear how many children are included in these numbers. Symptoms are most pronounced during the afternoon and evening hours.

Patient Age and Profile

Most children who have symptoms of SAD are able to benefit from phototherapy. Therapeutic success with patients who have premenstrual syndrome indicates that phototherapy may be particularly helpful for adolescent girls.

How the Technique Works

The human body naturally responds to earth's day/night cycles, according to researchers Richard and Judith Wurtman (1989). Light affects the production and functioning of hormones (such as melatonin, which influences mood and energy level) and neurotransmitters (such as serotonin, thought to be related to appetite and a sense of calm). Some people are particularly sensitive to the shortened daylight that comes with fall and winter. By simulating a longer daylight period, phototherapy alters the child's biological clock, countering by artificial means the unpleasant symptoms. However, Wurtman and Wurtman admit, "The mechanisms by which the therapy works remain a mystery."

A child undergoing phototherapy sits or sleeps under or next to the special light source for an amount of time ranging from thirty minutes to two hours daily during the low light seasons. Researchers report greater impact when the therapy takes place in the early morning hours of the day, and therefore interest has focused on use of a programmable dawn simulator. For children who have only mild symptoms, some therapists recommend a one-hour walk or outdoor play period during midday.

Definition

Phototherapy, also called light therapy, refers to the selective use of intense light to treat a wide range of physical and emotional symptoms. Although this technique is often employed in medical settings (for instance, in neonatal nurseries to treat jaundice), research since the 1980s supports its application to individuals suffering symptoms associated with Seasonal Affective Disorder (SAD). Phototherapy exposes the child or adolescent to concentrated, artificial light from which the dangerous ultraviolet rays of the spectrum are omitted. A minimum of thirty minutes per day of supplemental exposure to 10,000 lux—a measure of light equivalent to the sunlight on a cloudy day in northern Europe—has been shown to reduce symptoms of depression, lethargy, and carbohydrate craving within days of beginning treatment.

Indicators/Measures of Success

Relief from symptoms is the clearest measure of success. Youngsters for whom phototherapy works report relief within one week of starting treatment and continue to feel better for up to a week after treatment stops. Lack of time is a factor in noncompliance.

Suggested Readings and Resources

Lam, Raymond, M.D., University of British Columbia/VHHSC Mood Disorders Clinic: "Info about Seasonal Affective Disorder." 2/98.

http://www.psychiatry.ubc.ca/mood/md_sad.html.

Wurtman, Richard, and Judith Wurtman. "Carbohydrates and Depression." *Scientific American*, January 1989, 68-75.

Poetry Therapy

When to Use the Technique

Case studies appearing across a range of professional journals indicate that poetry therapy is useful for patients with bipolar emotional disturbances, with adolescent ego- and ethnic-identity conflicts, and with a history of sexual abuse, among other problems. Lerner (1982) recommends having poetry therapy groups in hospitals, in correction facilities and other institutional settings, and in private practice.

Patient Age and Profile

Although the professional literature on poetry therapy addresses primarily adolescents and older patients, younger children do write and relate to poetry. Decisions on using poetry in therapy with younger patients are best left to the therapist.

How the Technique Works

Poetry therapy depends on the emotional appeal inherent in this expressive art form to provide information, to elicit response and self-disclosure, and to highlight difficulties and strengths. It offers linkages between the inner being and the external world. Poetry therapy is conducted in a nonjudgmental context, and trust is an essential component.

In poetry therapy groups, participants sit facing each other in a circle, with ample supplies of paper, writing tools, poetry books, and copies of poems representing a wide variety of emotions and issues. Lerner suggests that a "poetry facilitator"—someone who has a special feel for poetry—may team with the therapist. His groups typically include seven to twelve people and run for one hour.

The session is conducted much like any group therapy session, with poetry as a springboard for exploring problematic themes, attitudes, and feelings. A poem can be provided to start the conversation, participants can be asked to bring in their favorite poem, or the participants can write for a few minutes on a particular type of event in their lives. Participants share experiences and responses; they improve their skills at communication and interaction and learn that they are not alone. Lerner

Definition

Poetry therapy refers to the adjunct use of poetry in a therapeutic setting. Practitioners distinguish poetry therapy from poetry workshops, noting that the former focuses on the person whereas the latter focuses more on the poetry. Poetry plays a number of roles in the healing processes in both individual and group therapy. As an expressive art, poetry can (1) serve as a catalyst to bring emotions to a higher level of awareness, (2) be a device for projection or symbolic communication, (3) validate feelings and experiences, and (4) promote insight into and discussion on problems relevant to the therapy.

noted that the therapist will gain information from these sessions, but he also cautioned that insight doesn't always translate into remedy and action.

Indicators/Measures of Success

Poetry therapy can encourage the expression of unwanted emotions. It can also call attention to the disparity between what a patient feels and how that patient actually relates to people in his or her everyday environment. The therapist needs to be alert and sensitive to these insights and help the patient move constructively with them.

Suggested Readings and Resources

Lerner, Arthur. "Poetry Therapy in the Group Experience." In Lawrence Abt and Irving Stuart, eds. *The Newer Therapies: A Sourcebook* (New York: Van Nostrand Reinhold Company Inc., 1982).

Technique

Progressive Muscle Relaxation

When to Use the Technique

This process can be used alone or in conjunction with a broader stress management or relaxation program. It is especially useful when physical symptoms of anxiety are also present.

Patient Age and Profile

The guided sequence of progressive muscle relaxation makes it appealing for less focused or younger children who need more structure or concrete instruction in learning how to relax.

How the Technique Works

The child is taught control over as many as sixteen different muscle groups. Although there are different approaches, the child typically starts with muscle groups at the extremities (feet or hands) and gradually moves up through the body toward the head (and sometimes back toward the extremities again). The child practices tensing or flexing the muscle tightly, holding the contraction for about six seconds, then relaxing it. The process is not rushed.

Indicators/Measures of Success

To the extent that anxiety is exacerbated by muscular tension, this technique can break the cycle. One obvious measure of success would therefore be in the increasing control gained by the child over his or her muscle tension and anxiety level. Less dramatic, but also important, might be the increasing ability of the child to respond to other relaxation and stress-reduction interventions.

Suggested Readings and Resources

Benson, Herbert. *The Relaxation Response.* New York: William Morrow and Company, 1975.

Rozensky, Ronald. "Biofeedback Training with Children." In Charles Schaefer, ed. *Innovative Interventions in Child and Adolescent Therapy* (New York: John Wiley & Sons, 1988).

Definition

Progressive muscle relaxation is a relaxation technique through which a child gains systematic control over specific muscle groups. It is based on the link between skeletal-muscle tension and emotional distress.

Prosocial Learning

When to Use the Technique

It is beneficial to use this technique whenever a child is "caught in the act of being good." His or her actions should be reinforced by saying something such as, "I saw you share your bike with Bobby. That was a really nice thing to do, and I felt proud of you." Children who are oppositional, aggressive, or have other behavior problems can be taught to be prosocial so that the focus is on positive behaviors rather than negative ones. Shapiro (1994) advocates teaching prosocial learning as part of a short-term therapy plan for the following reasons:

- It redirects adults from the problem behavior toward a behavior that can be accomplished fairly easily. It is always easier to teach a new positive behavior than to extinguish a negative one.

- It changes the child's mode of functioning and can have important side effects for other family members.

- The child builds a platform for his or her self-esteem: the experiences make the child feel good, and he or she is praised for good work and concern for others.

Patient Age and Profile

Children of all ages can benefit from this technique.

How the Technique Works

Reinforcing prosocial behavior with praise should be part of a program that includes "prosocial assignments," stimulated by the child's empathy for others. The child should be instructed on how to carry out these assignments and be made cognizant of other good models (such as the child's parent). The child should also be taught prosocial values.

Social action includes things that people do that extend beyond their own home or classroom into the "real world." Examples of realistic prosocial activities for children include writing letters to facilitate change, volunteering for local charities, doing work to change and improve the environment, lobbying for causes, and so on. "These are things that are not required of you," writes Barbara Lewis in *The Kid's*

Definition

The word "prosocial" refers to any action that a person takes in order to benefit someone else. Prosocial learning includes sharing, helping, protecting, giving aid and comfort, befriending, showing affection, and giving encouragement. It also focuses on "selfless" tasks, such as doing volunteer work for charity or doing something to help the environment.

Guide to Social Action. "You don't *have* to do them. You do them selflessly, to improve the quality of life around you."

Indicators/Measures of Success

Lewis counsels children, "Solving social problems will bring excitement and suspense into your life. Instead of reading dusty textbooks and memorizing what other people have done, you'll create your own history with the actions you take…As you reach out to solve problems in your community, you'll be helping to design a better future. You'll also be learning to take charge of your personal life. You'll become more confident in yourself because you'll prove to yourself that you can do almost anything."

Suggested Readings and Resources

Lewis, Barbara. *The Kid's Guide to Social Action.* Minneapolis: Free Spirit Press, 1991.

Schulman, Michael, and Eva Mekler. *Bringing Up a Moral Child.* New York: Doubleday, 1994.

Shapiro, Lawrence E. *Short-term Therapy with Children.* Plainview, NY: Childswork/Childsplay, 1994.

Psychodrama

Definition

In psychodrama, children are invited to participate in role playing and skits in which they reenact relevant and sometimes painful aspects of their own histories. As a character in the play, the therapist can model the verbal expression of feelings or ask how the child's character feels.

When to Use the Technique

Like role playing, psychodrama provides the child with distance from his or her distress. Just as hiding behind a puppet theater and speaking as a puppet can ease anxiety, so too can dressing up in costumes and pretending to be someone else offer a sense of relief for anxious or traumatized children.

Patient Age and Profile

Most young children can be enticed to join in the drama when the therapist presents hats, sunglasses, masks, scarves, costumes, and so on to create spontaneous "productions" that serve to enhance the child's sense of psychological safety. Other props, such as toy telephones, can allow the child to "talk" to someone he or she is not yet ready to face directly.

James (1989) writes that young teenagers have chosen to sit quietly and discuss their concerns when both the teen and therapist were playing character roles, and whole families have dressed up and created dramas in which everyone contributed to the direction of the action.

How the Technique Works

In James' psychodramatic intervention, the therapist tells the child, "Today, you're the director. Tell me what role you would like me to play. Do we need to use any dolls? How do we begin?" or "Today let's do a play about a little forest creature who is lost and can't find its parents. What role would you like to play?" The therapist could suggest taking some ideas from the child's former sand play or drawings and creating a short skit.

James also discusses a variation of psychodrama that she calls "clowning." Given the premise that clowns have permission to do "almost anything," the child has clown makeup put on him or her, which fosters safe touching, eye contact, and a shared creative experience. Whiteface is not advised for small children because they often experience this as a fearful loss of identity; colors are fun for them, always with a red circle on the nose.

Indicators/Measures of Success

James writes, "The therapist enters the world of the child, where communication is conducted in the child's own language. Children as animals, heroes, and fairy princesses are able to play out their conflicts, speak the unspeakable, display emotions and behaviors that have been blocked, practice new ways of being, and demonstrate their hurts and wishes" (p. 209). James' clowning technique allows emotional freedom, is fun, and provides a safe way for the child to be silly, mean, tricky, or sad.

Suggested Readings and Resources

James, Beverly. *Treating Traumatized Children: New Insights and Creative Interventions.* New York: Free Press, 1989.

Pearce, James, and Terry Pezzot-Pearce. *Psychotherapy with Abused and Neglected Children.* New York: The Guilford Press, 1997.

Technique

Purposeful Interviewing

When to Use the Technique

The questions in this process are targeted toward helping families get "unstuck" so that they may move forward in working on problems.

Patient Age and Profile

Selekman (1993) recommends this process for use in brief therapy with difficult adolescents and their families and for families who are entrenched and/or traumatized as well.

How the Technique Works

Selekman writes, "The various interventive questions...can promote self-healing and liberate families from their oppressive problems by opening up space for new possibilities" (p. 54). The categories of questions include:

- **Pretreatment change questions,** such as, "So what have you noticed that's better since you first called our clinic?" not only convey the idea that the therapist believes that the family has the strength and resources to change but also presuppose that changes have already occurred, which can help set in motion the creation of a positive self-fulfilling prophecy for the family.

- **"Why now" questions,** such as, "What brings you in now?" and "What would you like to change today (or first)?" help the therapist set treatment goals, determine what led the family to therapy, and ascertain what the members want to work on changing first.

- **Exception-oriented questions** can serve to actively disrupt the family's problem-talk interactive pattern. Examples include, "You have given me a fairly good picture of the problem, but in order to have a more complete picture I need to know more. When this problem is not happening, what is happening instead?" and "If we asked Bill, what would he say he would want the two of you [the parents] to continue doing that was helping you get along better?"

- **Unique account and redescription questions** assist families in the co-authoring of new stories about themselves and their relationships that counter the dominant stories that have been oppressing them.

Definition

Purposeful interviewing is a process used in solution-oriented therapy where the therapist asks questions in a purposeful manner and carefully assesses a family's cooperative response pattern, matching questions with those patterns (de Shazer, 1991).

"How did you manage to take this important step to turn things around?" and "What were you telling yourself to get ready for this big step?" are examples of unique account questions.

Examples of unique redescription questions are, "What does this tell you about yourself that is important to know?" and "How has this new picture of yourself changed how you view yourself as a person?" These questions "invite family members to ascribe significance and new meaning to the exceptions and unique accounts through the redescription of themselves, their family relationships, and significant others."

- **Presuppositional questions** (O'Hanlon and Weiner-Davis, 1989) are powerful interventive questions that can be utilized to amplify pretreatment changes and exceptions, to convey the inevitability of change to clients, to elicit the client's outcome goal, and to co-create a future client reality without problems. Examples include, "How will you know when you won't have to come here anymore?" "What will you be doing differently over the next week?" and "What will a small sign of progress look like in the next week that will indicate to you that you are heading in the right direction?"

- **Miracle questions** (de Shazer) serve to rapidly move clients into a future reality without problems, such as, "Suppose the three of you go home tonight and while you are asleep a miracle happens and your problem is solved. What will be different?" (See "The Miracle Question" in Volume I of *The Therapist's Toolbox*.)

- **Coping questions** are for families that do not respond well to miracle questions. They are meant to mirror their pessimistic stance by asking, "How come things aren't worse?"

- **Scaling questions** (de Shazer) are useful for securing a quantitative measurement of the family problem prior to treatment, presently, and where they would like to be in one week's time. Once the family has identified and rated the problem situation on a scale of 1 to 10, the therapist's job is to negotiate with the parents and adolescent on what each party will have to do to get at least a half to a whole point higher on the scale in one week's time. For example, "Where would you rate Marie's behavior today?" (Mother says "6.") "What would Marie have to do to bring this up to a 7?"

- **Pessimistic questions** are asked if parents continue to insist that their adolescent's behaviors will continue to get worse and produce dire consequences. Examples are, "What do you think will happen if things don't get better?" "Who will suffer the most?" and "What do you suppose is the smallest thing you could do that might make a slight difference?" These questions might help parents remember past successful parenting strategies that they can use with the current crisis.

- **Externalizing questions** serve to externalize a presenting problem that has fallen into a pattern. Examples include, "How long has this 'blaming' pattern been pushing all of you around?" and "Do you see how blaming got in between the two of you and made you lock horns with each other?"

- **Future-oriented questions** are based on the notion that the future is fertile ground for change because it has not happened yet. Selekman reports that research indicates that those individuals who can envision a future of mastery and success at performing tasks will tend to outperform those who anticipate failure. Examples of future-oriented questions are, "When Johnny gets a job, who will be the most surprised in the family?" and "What else will be different?"

- **Problem-tracking questions**, such as, "If you were to show me a videotape of how things look when your brother comes home drunk, who confronts him first, your mother or father?" help the therapist secure a detailed picture from family members regarding the specific family patterns that have resulted in the presenting problem being maintained.

- **Conversational questions** are open-ended and are the narrative therapist's primary tool for helping to keep the therapeutic conversation going. Examples include, "What do you suppose the other therapists you have seen overlooked or missed with you?" "If there were one question you were hoping I might ask, what would that be?" and "Who in the family will have the most difficulty talking about this issue?"

- **Consolidating questions** are useful for amplifying pretreatment changes and for reinforcing family changes that occur in second and subsequent sessions: "What will you have to continue to do to keep these changes happening?" "How will you get back on track again if you have a landslide?" and "If we were to gaze into my crystal ball three weeks down the road, what further changes would we see happening?"

Indicators/Measures of Success

Families can be empowered with this interview approach. Through the use of purposeful questions, the gains family members have made can be reinforced through amplification, consolidation, and validation by the therapist. When families are reassured that even small changes are significant, they become empowered in tackling bigger issues. Visualization of future success can in itself be a catalyst toward future goal attainment.

Suggested Readings and Resources

de Shazer, Steve. *Putting Difference to Work.* New York: Norton, 1991.

O'Hanlon, William, and M. Weiner-Davis. *In Search of Solutions: A New Direction in Psychotherapy.* New York: Norton, 1989.

Selekman, Matthew. *Pathways to Change: Brief Therapy Solutions with Difficult Adolescents.* New York: The Guilford Press, 1993.

Technique

Reattachment Therapy

When to Use the Technique

Reattachment therapy is used to improve situations when bonding has been disrupted by trauma or abuse. In cases where the parent is receiving therapy for aggressive or abusive behavior, reattachment therapy focuses on the child's role, modifying inappropriate behaviors that tend to perpetuate the cycle of abuse.

Patient Age and Profile

Reattachment therapy targets very young children under age 6 who have been physically abused. These youngsters can learn to control antisocial behaviors that tend to alienate and exasperate their primary (abusive) caretakers.

How the Technique Works

Several steps are involved in this intervention (Schaefer et al., 1986). The therapist begins by re-creating a sense of trust and unconditional bonding with the child so that he or she can associate adults with positive nurturing.

The therapist then attempts to modify some of the provocative aspects of the child's behavior or appearance and to reinforce those qualities and actions that induce attachment, such as smiling and making eye contact. The child's strengthened repertoire contributes to reattachment by breaking part of the pattern that had reinforced abuse.

Indicators/Measures of Success

A decrease in behaviors that provoke aggression is one measure of the child's response to therapy. However, reattachment involves the responsiveness of other people besides the youngster and includes many variables that may be beyond the scope of this intervention.

Suggested Readings and Resources

Frazier, D., and E. LeVine. "Reattachment Therapy: Intervention with the Very Young Physically Abused Child." *Psychotherapy*, 20: 90-100.

Miermont, Jacques, and Hugh Jenkins. *A Dictionary of Family Therapy*. Oxford, England: Blackwell Publishers, 1995.

Schaefer, Charles, Howard Millman, Steven Sichel, and Jane Zwilling, eds. *Advances in Therapies for Children* (San Francisco: Jossey-Bass, 1986).

Definition

A healthy bonding relationship between a child and his or her parent/parent-substitute is significant for survival and development. Reattachment therapy attempts to build or restore bonding between a child and a primary caretaker.

The Reflecting Team

When to Use the Technique

This brief therapy intervention works well with families that are "stuck" therapeutically and for therapists who feel "stuck" in helping a particular family.

Patient Age and Profile

All family members can benefit from this technique.

How the Technique Works

If the clinic has a one-way mirror or closed-circuit TV, midway through the session the interviewing therapist and the family can switch rooms with the consultation team, and they can listen to and watch the team's conversation about the family's problem. After the team's six- to nine-minute conversation, the therapist and family switch rooms again, and the family responds to the team's reflections. The family may elect to have the reflecting team in the same room during the entire session. Another variation is to have a colleague in the therapy room, sitting close to the interviewing therapist, and the family in the observing position. Midway through the session the two therapists have their reflection in front of the family. The family then reflects on the therapists' conversation.

When reflecting, Selekman (1997) suggests that therapists:

- Begin reflections with qualifiers such as, "I wonder if...?" "Could it be that...?"and "What struck me is that..."

- Avoid bombarding the family with too many ideas.

- Avoid pushing for team consensus with ideas.

- Keep reflections short and to the point.

- Avoid pathologizing language or negative explanation that may be interpreted as blaming by family members.

- Be careful not to make excessive use of positive relabeling (minimizing the situation). Family members may think you are being sarcastic or trying to talk them out of their problems.

Definition
The reflecting team usually includes a group of professionals who are impartial and objective and who preferably do not know the history of the family being treated. However, just one colleague can also act as a reflecting "team."

- Include the interviewing therapist as part of the themes or events on which you are reflecting.

- Be curious about the missing pieces of the family puzzle, including potential family secrets or the "not yet said," which you can carefully wonder about out loud with the team.

- Keep reflections from being too similar or too far removed from how the family views their problem story.

Indicators/Measures of Success

If the reflecting team method results in the discovery of alternative views or explanations of the problem and the events that led up to it, then the technique can be deemed successful. The experience should help the family and therapist to view themselves, their actions, and their relationships differently. The reflecting team models other ways for the problem to be resolved, with no one view being any more "correct" than any other (Andersen, 1991). This experience also teaches the family that their problem story is not carved in stone but is in constant evolutionary flux. The reflections by the team are meant to be "liberating," not corrective or prescriptive.

Selekman writes, "The major strength of the reflecting team is that it creates a learning climate that celebrates differences, which increases the likelihood for new ideas and meanings to be internalized by family members. A good team reflection can have a liberating effect for the stuck interviewing therapist, helping him or her get out of treatment impasses, gain access to fresh ideas, and discover more effective ways to cooperate with family members."

Suggested Readings and Resources

Andersen, T. *The Reflecting Team: Dialogues and Dialogues About the Dialogues.* New York: Norton, 1991.

Selekman, Matthew. *Solution-Focused Therapy with Children.* New York: The Guilford Press, 1997.

Rituals in Therapy

When to Use the Technique

Hoorwitz shows that rituals can help block unproductive behaviors that tend to maintain problems. He cites cases where rituals have successfully countered hallucinations and suicidal inclinations, as well as separation anxiety and headaches among young children.

Patient Age and Profile

Ritualistic interventions are particularly effective for children under age twelve because their cognitive development is still in the magical, prescientific stage. Patients of any age under stress are also amenable to this technique because their emotional turmoil may cause them to revert to less developed thinking (Hoorwitz).

How the Technique Works

Anthropology finds rituals to be a significant aspect of the healing process among countless prescientific cultures. One principle underlying the tool is the patient's naïve belief in the cause-effect relationship between the ritual and some desired event. Hoorwitz (1988) explains that ritual interventions depend on magical thinking to "depotentiate" the child's conscious, critical scrutiny of the "dubious causal link." Belief is rooted in the incomprehensibility and mystery surrounding the rituals. The fanfare or routines accompanying the rituals help distract the believer from logical strategies, thereby promoting a new perspective on the problem. Without use of logical reasoning then, a child can link the squeezing of a doll with the exorcism of internal voices (Hoorwitz, 1988), just as some cultures link the sticking of a voodoo doll with injury to another person.

Therapeutic rituals include the principles of imitation, contagion (transference), and symmetry or polarity (balancing evil with good). The specific rituals, including traditional rites of passage, can effect a change in the family's relationships. Therapists prescribe rituals to coincide with symbols and values that are significant to the child and his or her family (to lend validity to the ritual), noting points in family development at which the child seems to be stuck.

Definition

Rituals can be used to promote healing when a child believes that particular sequences or acts produce particular effects. Ritualistic interventions are crafted to coincide with developmental stages of children and to halt ineffective efforts by families to resolve ongoing problems (Hoorwitz, 1988).

A simple example shows how ritual was used to allay one four-year-old's severe anxiety after the separation of her parents. The girl's father cooperated in establishing a special routine for hugging a particular stuffed animal, which he told her would stay with her and would remind her of how much he loved her and was thinking of her.

Indicators/Measures of Success

Case studies show a fairly immediate (though often temporary) response to the ritualistic intervention, as well as a longer-term empowering of children and their families to deal with the problematic issues if they recur. The success may actually be related to the appearance of additional agents of change that the use of ritual has opened to the family (Hoorwitz).

Suggested Readings and Resources

Hoorwitz, Aaron N. "The Therapeutic Use of Rituals with Children." Charles Schaefer, ed. *Innovative Interventions in Child and Adolescent Therapy* (New York: John Wiley & Sons, 1988).

Rock Music to Reduce Hyperactivity

When to Use the Technique

This technique is particularly useful in classroom-type settings with youngsters who have attention deficits and hyperactivity but who are supposed to focus on completing specified tasks. Background music is a relatively simple intervention that can be played for a group over a speaker system or targeted to individuals wearing headphones.

Patient Age and Profile

This technique has been used with children aged five and older who have impulsivity with attention deficit hyperactivity disorder.

How the Technique Works

There is research evidence that popular background music with a strong beat helps reduce hyperkinesis and contributes to accomplishing various academic and motor tasks.

Children who have hyperactivity perform certain tasks better and engage in fewer disruptive and distracting activities when rhythmic instrumental music is played in the background (Scott, 1970; Burleson, et al. 1989).

Researchers are not certain exactly why the background beat has a calming and efficacious impact, but there are hypotheses. These hypotheses reject the notion that hyperactivity results from an overstimulating environment. Instead, hyperactive children are believed to have *under*stimulated areas of the brain (accounting for below-typical levels of beta waves and above-average alpha wave activity). The rock music stimulates these children enough to allow them to block out distractions and concentrate more on a single task.

Indicators/Measures of Success

One obvious indication of success of this technique would be if it indeed facilitates higher productivity and less distractibility in a child. Some experimentation with the type of beat and the length of time it plays

Definition

This technique uses the rhythms of rock music to help hyperactive children focus and concentrate better on tasks. It is an adjunctive therapy to help manage the behavioral consequences of the problem (Cripe, 1986).

may be warranted.

Suggested Readings and Resources

Burleson, S., D. Center, and H. Reeves. "Effect of Background Music on Task Performance in Psychotic Children." *Journal of Music Therapy*, 26(4).

Cripe, F. "Rock Music as Therapy for Children with Attention Deficit Disorder: An Exploratory Study." *Journal of Music Therapy*, Spring, 23(1): 30-37.

Scott, Thomas. "The Use of Music to Reduce Hyperactivity in Children." *American Journal of Orthopsychiatry*, 40: 677-680. In Charles Schaefer and Howard Millman, eds. *Therapies for Children* (San Francisco: Jossey-Bass, 1977).

Self-Control Training

When to Use the Technique

Although in a general sense all children benefit from learning self-control, this technique is intended for children with conduct disorders, fears, and other maladaptive cognitive problems that impede healthy development.

Patient Age and Profile

Children aged five and older can be given self-control training to alter their self-defeating patterns and to control impulsive or other inappropriate responses.

How the Technique Works

Self-control training actually subsumes many techniques that target different aspects of functioning. It incorporates cognitive restructuring, role play, modeling, problem-solving, self-instruction, behavior assignments, self-evaluation, and self-reinforcement. The child actively participates all through the process, which presumably contributes to gains in self-esteem and mastery over problems.

Indicators/Measures of Success

Indications that this training is working include reduction in problem behaviors by the child and greater success in facing challenging situations in his or her regular environment.

Suggested Readings and Resources

Kanfer, Frederick, and Bruce Schefft. *Guiding the Process of Therapeutic Change.* Champaign, Illinois: Research Press, 1988.

Stark, Kevin, Lawrence Rouse, and Ronald Livingston. "Treatment of Depression During Childhood and Adolescence: Cognitive-Behavioral Procedures for the Individual and Family." In Philip Kendall, ed. *Child and Adolescent Therapy.* (New York: The Guilford Press, 1991).

Definition

Self-control training attempts to give a child the skills and understanding necessary to control problematic symptoms and behaviors. It helps a child to regulate his or her behavior, to cease doing certain things that have become automatic responses, or start to do certain things that he or she was reluctant to do before.

Technique

Self-Modeling

Definition

Self-modeling is a special application of the modeling process [see pp. 103 to 104] with particular emphasis on using the child's own successes as the behavior to reinforce and replicate.

When to Use the Technique

Self-modeling has been used to modify extreme social withdrawal and shyness. Dowrick (1979) applied self-modeling in conjunction with a single dose of medication to create a carefully edited self-model video to overcome social isolation. He believes success in this case was due to the combination of medication with the self-modeling process and recommends this approach for school phobias and performance anxiety in children.

Patient Age and Profile

In the example presented by Dowrick, the child was five years old and exhibited extraordinary shyness.

How the Technique Works

Self-modeling, like modeling, provides positive examples for the child to imitate. However, instead of relying on other people to provide the cues, self-modeling empowers the youngster with the concrete vision of him- or herself executing the desirable behaviors.

Videotapes created by Dowrick contained enhancements, repetitions, and serious editing to achieve the behaviors he wanted to reinforce and teach. In the case reported, one of the videotapings coincided with the use of a single dose of Valium to decrease the child's extreme shyness. The child then viewed a short video segment twice each week over a period of several weeks, during which time he participated in structured, cooperative play activities with one peer and a therapist.

The therapist was quite selective in creating and editing the videotape that supported the child's social initiatives. The child's interactions not only improved during the course of therapy but also continued throughout the follow-up year after therapy had terminated.

Indicators/Measures of Success

In the case studied, the child moved well beyond the limited (even contrived) social approaches captured and enhanced in the videos. There was no need for medication after the initial session. The child's acquired social behaviors not only endured over time but also generalized to social contexts outside of those modeled in the videos or practiced in therapy sessions.

Suggested Readings and Resources

Dowrick, P. W. "Single-Dose Medication to Create a Self-Model Film." *Child Behavior Therapy,* l(2): 193-198. Discussed in Charles Schaefer, Howard Millman, Steven Sichel, and Jane Zwilling, eds. *Advances in Therapies for Children* (San Francisco: Jossey-Bass Publishers, 1986).

Technique

Self-Reinforcement Training

When to Use the Technique

Self-reinforcement is part of a larger program that teaches self-control. It is used in combination with self-instruction, self-evaluation or self-monitoring, cognitive restructuring, modeling, and other techniques.

Patient Age and Profile

This technique is used with children as young as five for problems of depression, dependency, anxiety, impulsivity, and other disorders.

How the Technique Works

Working collaboratively, the therapist and child draw up a menu of pleasant incentives, within the child's control (and/or with the cooperation of parents), with which he or she could self-reward progress. These rewards are ranked on a basis of potency to correspond to increasingly difficult or demanding tasks. Homework between therapy sessions involves practicing the therapeutic tasks, together with self-talk, self-evaluation, and appropriate self-reinforcement.

Preparing a child to use self-reinforcement sometimes includes practice with the therapist in learning how to self-evaluate. The child practices evaluating his or her own behavior or coping skill, seeing how closely it matches that of the therapist. This process helps guide the child toward realistic and positive self-ratings on which self-reinforcement is based.

Indicators/Measures of Success

The success of this technique is measured by the child's progress in developing and maintaining the desired skills and behaviors.

Suggested Readings and Resources

Kendall, Philip, and Lauren Braswell. *Cognitive Behavioral Therapy for Impulsive Children*. New York: The Guilford Press, 1993.

Stark, Kevin, Lawrence Rouse, and Ronald Livingston. "Treatment of Depression During Childhood and Adolescence: Cognitive-Behavioral Procedures for the Individual and Family." In Philip Kendall, ed. *Child and Adolescent Therapy* (New York: The Guilford Press, 1991).

Definition

Self-reinforcement training is designed to help a child reward him- or herself for improving or accomplishing desirable behaviors. It motivates the child to continue practicing newly acquired strategies and gives the child a sense of control.

Sensory and Regressive Play

When to Use the Technique

This technique is used with youngsters who have suffered trauma, prolonged illness, severe deprivation, abuse, or other experiences that denied them developmental opportunities and nurturing. The child is not merely "left" to engage in regressive play but is nurtured along as one might with a younger child in order to progress to a higher stage of development.

Patient Age and Profile

Very young children can benefit from this technique. It is not clear from the professional literature at exactly what age this approach might cease to be useful.

How the Technique Works

There are several approaches with this kind of play. One is nondirected, in which the child gives instructions to the therapist/playmate, using the mother-baby relationship as the focus. This play may include cuddling, rocking, and sometimes feeding. Occasionally therapists report dialogue that seems to reenact scenes from the child's background.

Another approach in using this technique is targeted to what McMahon (1992) calls "unfreezing the senses." Too often, these children have never appropriately explored the world with their senses, and these areas of their bodies are undereducated. Therefore, the therapist works with these children to broaden their feelings, their vocabulary, and their experience in the areas of sound, touch, smell, sight, and even taste.

For example, the therapist might play a tape and ask the child to guess the sounds on it. The sounds may range from water dripping to a car motor backfiring, and the child would practice describing the feeling he or she gets when listening to that sound. The child could also learn to discriminate between angry, sad, and worried tones of voice, and reflect these moods with musical instruments.

Definition

Sensory and regressive play encourages a child to return to a form of play that is developmentally below his or her age level in order to recapture some of the experiences and deficits that were missed earlier in the child's life.

Indicators/Measures of Success

The goal of this technique is for the child to become better acquainted with his or her body and feelings, to gain self-esteem and confidence, and to be in a stronger position to bond with and relate to other human beings. Progress would be measured by enhanced interaction and ability to connect.

Suggested Readings and Resources

McMahon, Linnet. *The Handbook of Play Therapy.* London: Routledge, 1992.

West, J. "Play Therapy with Rosy." *British Journal of Social Work,* 13: 645-661. Discussed in Garry Landreth, L. Homeyer, G. Glover, and D. Sweeney, eds. *Play Therapy Interventions with Children's Problems* (Northvale, N.J.: Jason Aronson, 1996).

Serial Drawing

When to Use the Technique

The technique is well suited for traumatized children who have been physically or sexually abused.

Patient Age and Profile

School-aged children benefit most from this intervention. It is often used in the office of a school counselor.

How the Technique Works

The theoretical underpinnings of this approach are based on the work of Carl Jung. To Jung, the expressive arts represented an important avenue to the inner world of feelings and images. Jung came to see the unconscious mind not only as a repository of repressed emotions but also as a source of health and transformation. He emphasized the importance of viewing children's drawings "in series" over time rather than analyzing one or two pictures.

There are three main stages in serial drawing. In the initial stage (first to fourth session), the drawings seem to give a view of the child's internal world, often showing images that hint at a cause of the child's problem and reflect the loss of internal control as well as feelings of despair and hopelessness. The images also offer a vehicle for the counselor to establish a rapport with the child. The counselor is often depicted in the drawings as a friendly figure, such as a pilot, doctor, or nurse.

In the middle stage (fifth to eighth session), the drawings seem to express an emotion in its pure form and depict the struggle between opposites (good vs. bad), with any accompanying ambivalent feelings. The relationship between the child and the helper deepens during this time. At the end of this phase, the child often uses the drawing as a bridge to talk openly about a painful issue or to disclose a secret.

In the termination stage (ninth to twelfth session), the child tends to draw images that reflect a sense of mastery, self-control, and worth.

Definition

Serial drawing is a therapeutic approach whereby a therapist meets on a regular basis with a child and simply asks the child to draw a picture. Over time, a relationship is formed, problems are expressed symbolically in the drawings, and healing and resolution of inner conflicts can occur. The piece of white paper becomes the safe place onto which projections are placed, while the symbols and images become the "containers" for various emotions, thus allowing feelings to be expressed safely. Fantasies and images are produced that, if expressed in tangible form through drawing, facilitate psychological growth.

Scenes often contain positive imagery and a central symbol of the self. Some scenes may be humorous or reflect the breaking of the attachment bond between the child and the helper.

At the end of each session, the counselor asks the child, "Does the picture tell a story? Can you tell me what's going on in the picture? Does the picture have a title? What went on in the story before this picture? What happens next?" If the child has spent a lot of time on one area of the drawing, the reason(s) for this attention should also be explored.

Serial drawing uses three main approaches:

Nondirective. Some children come to the sessions, see the paper and pencil, and start drawing before the counselor can talk. These children readily respond to the therapeutic environment and seem to know what they want to draw. It is important to use a nondirective approach with these children because they are connected to their own curative process.

Directive. Some children seem withdrawn, stuck, confused, and very uncertain of themselves. Often a suggestion of what to draw helps these children get underway. The House-Tree-Person drawing can be a starting point until they are ready to draw on their own. The therapist should base the direction on what he or she assesses to be a central emotion that the child seems to be struggling with or a symbol or image that seems to have special meaning to the child.

Partially Directive. Sometimes one particular image has a special relevance to the child, such as a house, a flower, a tree, the sun, a cage, or a dog. In this approach, every four to six weeks the counselor asks the child to draw that particular symbol again, as it takes this long for the psyche to register change and the child to exhibit a slightly new attitude or relationship to the key symbol.

Indicators/Measures of Success

When children draw in the presence of the counselor on a regular basis, themes depicting trauma, transference, the struggle with ambivalent feelings, reparation, and healing are revealed. Many children use one main symbolic theme as the vehicle for change, and with counseling the symbol changes from the initial damaged form to one that reflects healthy functioning. The content of the drawing is often used as a bridge to direct verbal self-disclosures, and at the end of the intervention drawings tend to depict self-confidence, restoration of the lost object, humor, the experience of nurturance, and emerging independence.

Suggested Readings and Resources

Allan, John."Serial Drawing: A Jungian Approach with Children." In Charles Schaefer, ed. *Innovative Interventions in Child and Adolescent Therapy.* New York: John Wiley & Sons, 1988.

Jung, Carl. *Archetypes and the Collective Unconscious.* Princeton, NJ: Princeton University Press, 1959.

Technique

Show-That-I-Can Task (STIC)

When to Use the Technique

The STIC task is a standard tool used at the Anxiety Disorders Clinic of Temple University in Philadelphia, but it can be adapted to individual or group treatment of people with anxiety disorders.

Patient Age and Profile

The technique is used in the treatment of child and adolescent anxiety disorders.

How the Technique Works

The child begins therapy by learning to identify anxious feelings and the somatic responses to them. After each session the child takes home a Show-That-I-Can task. The first of these is to write down a brief example of a time when the child felt really great, not worried or upset. The child is then asked to try to think and focus on what made him or her comfortable and what was felt and thought at the time. To help the child understand the assignment, the therapist should provide an example of a time when he or she felt really great, describing it in terms of what was felt and thought. In the earlier sessions, when the task is completed, the child earns points, which can be used to purchase rewards such as small toys, books, or games. Later on, the rewards might be time spent playing a computer game or going out for ice cream with the therapist.

The STIC task is supplemented by activities such as role playing and storytelling, learning to use relaxation techniques and self-talk, and learning coping strategies. In the final sessions, children make a TV commercial in which their hero copes with a tense situation.

Indicators/Measures of Success

Homework assignments such as the Show-That-I-Can task can help reinforce what has been addressed during the therapy session. Success can be considered achieved if a child learns to recognize signs of unwanted anxious arousal and lets these signs serve as cues for the use of anxiety-management techniques.

Definition

The Show-That-I-Can (STIC) task is a method of teaching children how to identify anxious feelings and recognize the body's (somatic) responses to them.

Suggested Readings and Resources

Fishman, Katherine. *Behind the One-Way Mirror: Psychotherapy and Children.* New York: Bantam, 1995.

Kendall, Philip, ed. *Child & Adolescent Therapy: Cognitive-Behavioral Procedures.* New York: The Guilford Press, 1991.

Technique

Sing-a-Song Music Therapy

When to Use the Technique

This technique might be considered when children develop sudden phobic reactions to school or to doctor visits, when they need confidence, or when they need a greater sense of control.

Patient Age and Profile

Bankart and Bankart used this tool for a nine-year-old boy. They suggest that as long as an appropriate song is used (one that fits the problem), children of any age should be able to benefit from this technique.

How the Technique Works

The child learns how to focus on anxiety-producing images, which he or she then pairs against a song, selected not so much for its popularity but for its themes of courage and confidence building. The child practices singing the song, which serves as a competing response, when the anxiety occurs. The song then helps block the phobic symptoms.

Indicators/Measures of Success

The success of this approach can be measured by the decrease in symptoms.

Suggested Readings and Resources

Bankart, C., and B. Bankart. "The Use of Song Lyrics to Alleviate a Child's Fears." *Child and Family Behavior Therapy*, 5(4): 81-83.

Definition

Music is used in a variety of ways in therapy. One way is to teach the anxious child to sing a song as a coping strategy. (Bankart and Bankart, 1983).

The Sleep Diary

When to Use the Technique

This tool can be helpful in the treatment of children who are experiencing sleep disorders, including difficulty falling asleep, bedtime struggles, nighttime awakenings, insomnia, and nightmares.

Patient Age and Profile

Preschool children are most often helped with this tool in conjunction with other related interventions.

How the Technique Works

A sleep disturbance may represent an isolated problem, or it may become evident in the process of evaluating other behavioral or emotional problems (Schroeder and Gordon, 1991). Although there is no one solution for all sleep problems, the gathering of information about the sleep environment and parents' responses to the behavior can be helpful in alleviating symptoms.

Parents should be interviewed about the child's bedtime and settling to sleep patterns, waking at night patterns, daytime sleep patterns, daytime behavior, and family relationships and social life. Because parents may not relate all relevant information in the interview, the sleep diary can be helpful in understanding the nature of sleep problems (Lyman and Hembree-Kigin, 1994). For the initial evaluation, it is recommended that parents complete the diary for a two-week period to obtain a sufficient sample of sleep behavior. Ferber (1985) asserts that the importance of the sleep diary for assessing the problem and determining the effectiveness of treatment cannot be overemphasized. When parents are tired or have had a particularly bad night, their perception of the problem is not always an accurate reflection of the actual behavior.

Indicators/Measures of Success

Critics of sleep diaries have noted that some parents have difficulty completing the measure during the night, when there may be confusion concerning which parent will make the entries. Further, parents often underestimate the number of times their children soothe themselves back to sleep after awakening during the night. However, research

Definition

The sleep diary is a tool that can aid in the treatment of sleep disturbances. Completed by the parent(s), it is a nightly record of the sleeping and wakings of a child who is experiencing sleep problems.

generally supports the accuracy of sleep diaries. Studies have found that parent-completed diaries largely agree with videotapes made of sleep behavior, and interview and diary data correlate at approximately 70 percent (Elias et al., 1986).

Suggested Readings and Resources

Elias, M., N. Nicolson, C. Bora, and J. Johnston. "Sleep/Wake Patterns of Breast-fed Infants in the First Two Years of Life." *Pediatrics,* 77: 322-329.

Ferber, R. *Solve Your Child's Sleep Problems.* New York: Simon & Schuster, 1985.

Lyman, Robert, and Toni Hembree-Kigin. *Mental Health Interventions with Preschool Children.* New York: Plenum Press, 1994.

Schroeder, Carolyn, and Betty Gordon. *Assessment and Treatment of Childhood Problems: A Clinician's Guide.* New York: The Guilford Press, 1991.

Social Skills Training

When to Use the Technique

Because appropriate social skills empower children to respond better to their environment, social skills training is sometimes implemented as a preventative strategy, targeting youngsters at risk. Social skills training has been targeted for prevention of teen pregnancy and substance abuse, as well as for preparation for employment. Many therapists believe, also, that there is a strong link between social skills deficits and conduct disorders, delinquency, social isolation, and antisocial behaviors. Social skills training supports therapy addressing any of these problems.

Although the skills can be practiced and developed independently, a small group setting is considered the most "natural" context for working on them (LeCroy, 1994).

Patient Age and Profile

Children and adolescents are unable to apply behaviors they have never learned. Youngsters benefit from interventions that increase their competence, that offer them positive alternatives to destructive behaviors, and that provide opportunities to practice new skills. Better control in social situations sometimes promotes greater self-esteem, which in turn may stop antisocial behaviors.

How the Technique Works

Social skills training teaches a number of interpersonal skills that are needed by children and that are associated with successful social interactions. Some studies focus on a single skill at a time, such as eye contact, and apply a range of interventions—including didactic, video modeling, role playing, and homework assignments—to build and reinforce that skill. LeCroy identifies 11 fundamental social skills and develops treatment sessions around each one. These skills are:

- creating positive interactions (giving and receiving compliments);
- getting to know others (starting conversations);
- making requests (getting more of what you want);
- expressing your feelings directly;

Definition

Social skills training (similar to, and sometimes referred to as, structured skills therapy or social problem solving) is a structured, multifaceted effort to increase the repertoire of social behaviors accessible to a child in his or her interpersonal relations.

- getting out (how to say "no");

- asserting rights;

- identifying how others feel (the art of empathy);

- dealing with those in authority;

- responsible decision making (thinking about things);

- learning to negotiate (conflict resolution); and

- asking for help when needed.

Training in these skill areas involves discussing the utility of the skill, examining examples when the skill would have helped, modeling the skill, practicing the skill in role plays and in other contexts, doing extra assignments, and reviewing. Constructive feedback and social reinforcement are generally part of the process.

Indicators/Measures of Success

Improvements can be measured for the specific skills being taught. It is more difficult to measure how these skills transfer to other situations and how they are integrated into the child's overall social interactions. A number of studies report positive gains that remain for months and even several years after treatment stops; others are more cautious about the generalization of the skills learned.

Suggested Readings and Resources

Kazdin, Alan. *Treatment of Antisocial Behavior in Children and Adolescents*. Homewood, Illinois: The Dorsey Press, 1985.

LeCroy, Craig. "Social Skills Training." C. LeCroy, ed. *Handbook of Child and Adolescent Treatment Manuals* (New York: Lexington Books, 1994).

Schaefer, Charles, Howard Millman, Steven Sichel, and Jane Zwilling, eds. *Advances in Therapies for Children* (San Francisco: Jossey-Bass, 1986).

Structured Doll Play

When to Use the Technique

This tool can be particularly helpful when the problem centers around a specific event that occurred in the past and was of short duration.

Patient Age and Profile

According to James, this technique can be used with children aged two and older. It addresses anxiety, abuse, trauma, and other situations in which a child may have been burdened by excessive demands for his or her developmental age.

How the Technique Works

The child is presented with a set of dolls and sometimes a doll house or other relevant props. Using verbal statements and questions, the therapist helps direct the child into picturing a particular scenario. The therapist is often very specific, noting, for example, that one doll represents an uncle and another the uncle's nephew. A story is begun, which the child then completes using the dolls.

In hospitals, dolls are used for diagnostic and therapeutic purposes, for example, to explore the level of the child's understanding of his or her condition, to uncover areas of misunderstanding, and to relieve stress.

Indicators/Measures of Success

A number of variables influence the effectiveness of structured doll play, including the directives, the length of the session, and how realistic the materials look. Success can be judged by observing the release of anxiety in the child and by seeing him or her gain mastery over the problem situation.

Suggested Readings and Resources

Conn, Jacob. "The Treatment of Fearful Children." *American Journal of Orthopsychiatry*, 11: 744-752. Discussed in Charles Schaefer and Howard Millman, eds. *Therapies for Children* (San Francisco: Jossey-Bass, 1977).

Gaynard, L., J. Goldberger, and L. Laidley. "Use of Stuffed, Body-Outline Dolls with Hospitalized Children and Adolescents." *Children's Health Care*, Fall, 20(4): 216-224.

James, O'Dessie Oliver. *Play Therapy: A Comprehensive Guide*. Northvale, NJ: Jason Aronson, 1997.

Definition

Structured doll play began with the work of Melanie Klein in the 1920s (James, 1997) in which dolls were used as a nonthreatening way to help children deal with intense emotional situations. The technique provides specific toys and cues that help put the focus on particular relationships and problems.

Technique

Structured Fantasies

When to Use the Technique

Case studies employ structured fantasies in conjunction with other techniques to eliminate or diminish problematic behaviors such as aggressive acting out and fire setting. This approach has been applied in group settings, as well as with individuals.

Patient Age and Profile

Stawar used structured fantasies successfully to help a seven-year-old boy to stop setting fires. The technique has also been used with older children.

How the Technique Works

This technique can be adapted, depending on the needs and situations of the patient. Stawar's approach included the use of a fictional story, devised to give his young patient an alternative to setting fires and depicting how a role model would behave instead. Dolls were used to enact and repeat the fantasy. The patient was reinforced when he accurately retold the story and whenever the story hero behaved appropriately. Similar scenes were set up in realistic situations at home. Stawar believes that reinforcement during the story was an important part of the treatment.

Scheidler (1972) used a structured fantasy as a first step in group sessions with adolescents. The fantasy was devised to help participants relax and to encourage a "daydreamy" emotional mood that the members would share together. Prompts from the therapist would then deepen the children's discussion of problem experiences and inspire them to make connections they had not perceived earlier.

Indicators/Measures of Success

Assuming the structured fantasies are targeted at reducing problem behaviors, it is possible to monitor the frequency of these incidents in order to ascertain whether the technique is working and whether it has had an impact lasting beyond treatment.

Definition

Therapeutic structuring of fantasies can help a child work imaginatively with a problem and promote a child's cognitive control over his or her behavior (Stawar, 1976). The therapist provides a story or daydream that sets the stage for other interventions in dealing with undesirable behaviors. In the fantasy, the child is faced with a scenario similar to the ones that prompt his or her inappropriate behaviors. The fantasy, however, typically offers the child a view of him- or herself taking a positive alternative behavior instead of the one the therapist is trying to discourage. The fantasy is often repeated until the child internalizes the message.

Suggested Readings and Resources

Scheidler, Thomas. "Use of Fantasy as a Therapeutic Agent in Latency-Age Groups." *Psychotherapy: Theory, Research and Practice,* 9: 299-302. Discussed in Schaefer, Charles, Howard Millman, Steven Sichel, and Jane Zwilling, eds. *Advances in Therapies for Children* (San Francisco: Jossey-Bass, 1986).

Stawar, T. "Fable Mod: Operantly Structured Fantasies as an Adjunct in the Modification of Firesetting Behavior." *Behavior Therapy and Experimental Psychiatry,* 7: 285-287. Discussed in Charles Schaefer and Howard Millman, eds. *Therapies for Children* (San Francisco: Jossey-Bass, 1977).

Technique

Systematic Desensitization

When to Use the Technique

This technique has been effective in treating a wide range of behaviors involving fears (e.g., injections, dentists, darkness, dogs, taking tests), phobias, obsessions and compulsions, depression, selective mutism, and stuttering.

Patient Age and Profile

Children of school age and older are best suited for this technique.

How the Technique Works

Systematic desensitization with children consists of three basic steps: (1) training in deep muscle relaxation, (2) rank ordering of fearful situations from least to most distressing, and (3) having the child imagine each of the situations while in a relaxed state. This pairing of the relaxed state with images of the feared stimulus begins with the least distressing scene and ends with the most distressing one, with progression through the series being contingent on imagining a scene without undue discomfort. Typically, the child is not allowed to progress to a new hierarchy item until he or she feels comfortable with the prior item.

For the treatment to work, the child must be able to arrange the stimulus scenes in the order of the distress they cause, generate vivid images of those scenes, and detect subtle bodily changes in response to them. As a treatment for children's fears and anxieties, systematic desensitization does not directly instruct the child in the proper way to interact with the feared stimulus; it is assumed that the child already has this pattern in his or her repertoire.

Roberts and Gordon (1979) used systematic desensitization in treating a five-year-old girl who was experiencing nightmares and night terrors following an accident in which she was severely burned. They chose a series of ten magazine pictures to represent a desensitization hierarchy. The pictures depicted fires in a wide variety of settings and uses. The girl's mother showed these to her daughter and had her rate each picture on a "scariness" scale ranging from 1 (not scary at all) to 5 (very scary). After being exposed to a picture, the girl played with her favorite toys for

Definition

Systematic desensitization involves first training the child to respond in a way that is incompatible or detrimental to anxiety, then requiring him or her to imagine a hierarchy of anxiety-provoking scenes or to gradually confront the actual fear-evoking stimuli. The incompatible response used most often is muscle relaxation, but Schroeder and Gordon (1991) suggest that laughing (e.g, in response to imagining the feared monster dressed in red flannel underwear), engaging in play with toys or games, eating food, or interacting with a favorite person can also be used.

a few minutes. The exposure trials lengthened gradually from fifteen seconds to sixty seconds. Daily presentations of the hierarchy continued for three weeks until the girl reached the picture that was scariest for her and was able to rate it as a 1.

Indicators/Measures of Success

King et al. (1988) assert that relaxation and graduated stimulus presentations are especially successful with phobic reactions involving intense physiological responses and extreme avoidance, or in cases when it is not advisable to use more confrontational methods.

The child's fears and anxieties should be alleviated with proper use of this technique or in conjunction with other interventions. In the case of the five-year-old girl who was severely burned, her nightmares ceased during the desensitization phase, and she displayed no fearful reactions to fire-related stimuli. Her nightmares did not recur for six months of follow-up, during which time she had to return to the hospital once more for a skin-graft operation.

Suggested Readings and Resources

Hatzenbuehler, L., and H. Schroeder. "Desensitization Procedures in the Treatment of Childhood Disorders." *Psychological Bulletin*, 85: 831-844.

King, N., D. Hamilton, and T. Ollendick. *Children's Phobias: A Behavioral Perspective.* New York: John Wiley & Sons, 1988.

Morris, R., and Thomas Kratochwill. *Treating Children's Fears and Phobias: A Behavioral Approach.* Elmsford, NY: Pergamon Press, 1983.

Schroeder, Carolyn, and Betty Gordon. *Assessment and Treatment of Childhood Problems: A Clinician's Guide.* New York: The Guilford Press, 1991.

Talking to the Wizard

When to Use the Technique

This technique is helpful when a child is feeling extremely insecure about a particular situation.

Patient Age and Profile

Children aged four through ten can benefit most from this intervention, but positive self-talk is a technique that can be used for a lifetime.

How the Technique Works

Talking to the Wizard assumes that a child *knows* how to solve a problem and how to ignore negative self-talk, but that in the heat of the moment he or she doesn't apply that knowledge (Isaacs and Ritchey, 1989). The wise and rational Wizard inside seems to be better at dealing with other people's problems than his or her own. The authors suggest having the child pretend that it is, in fact, another child who has the problem, not he or she.

Citing the example of ten-year-old James, Isaacs and Ritchey portray him bursting through the door, raving to his mother about how he's "gonna kill" Bobby, the neighbor boy who "never" does what James wants him to do, who "always has to be the boss," and so on. When a child is that upset, Isaacs and Ritchey say, his or her parents must understand what happened before they can help the child get in touch with his or her Wizard. Asking leading questions, James's mother finally deduces that Bobby hadn't wanted to play a certain computer game but had gone along with James because he was so insistent. Bobby apparently got bored and just got up and left after a short while.

James's mother lets him cool down and reflects his feelings back to him, saying, "I can see how upset you are, James. You're not only mad, your feelings are hurt, too, because Bobby just left you there.... You know, I overheard you give Joe advice the other day when he was upset like this. Why don't you see if you can kind of step back and ask yourself, "'What would I tell Bobby if he had this problem?'"

Definition

This intervention allows a child to "talk to" the wise, rational part of himself or herself ("the Wizard") to solve problems and challenge negative self-talk.

Indicators/Measures of Success

Children can draw upon any positive model they have for a Wizard. A child may not be able to even *imagine* himself or herself speaking confidently, hitting a home run, or the like. The child may not be able to think of a past success and apply it to the current situation. But he or she will probably be able to tell you who *could* talk confidently or hit a home run. That model (or Wizard) might be a classmate, an older sibling, a TV or movie star, or a well-known athlete. If you can get the child to imagine how that model would handle the situation, that information could be used to guide the child's own thoughts, feelings, and behavior.

Suggested Readings and Resources

Isaacs, Susan, and Wendy Ritchey. *"I Think I Can, I Know I Can!"* New York: St. Martin's Press, 1989.

Technique

Telephone Play

When to Use the Technique

Telephone play should be used as a therapeutic aid and not as a substitute for other intensive therapy. It should be instituted with the full understanding of the child's changing levels of awareness, emotional flexibility, and insight.

Patient Age and Profile

Young children will be most amenable to this intervention.

How the Technique Works

The therapeutic value of toys lies mostly in the child's ability and desire to engage them in natural play, with a secondary effect being the communication of fantasy or information. Spero (1993) writes, "In play therapy, the telephone is readily assimilated by children wishing to fantasize, externalize affect, or express fears and frustrations.... A telephone conversation becomes a socially acceptable way for a child to acknowledge inner fears by articulating them in the guise of another party on the line."

Spero points out that the telephone is in itself an instrument of communication, and from the outset the child knows that it is a social instrument. It is also a potentially symbolic play object because it simultaneously combines talking and listening plus responding in ways not visible to the person at the other end of the line. For many children, the use of the telephone also symbolizes mastery of adult abilities, including manipulating the dial, conversing with friends, and doing two things at the same time.

In therapy, the telephone stimulates fantasy, encouraging a child to conduct a dialogue with an imaginary second party. Whom the child decides to call, what he or she says and "hears" the other person say, and what role he or she plays as the second party can reveal much information. When children use the telephone in the presence of the therapist, they intuitively assume the therapist's participation at the other end of the line. The telephone can also be used to fantasize a connection with someone who is dead or lives far away. In this situation, the child's

Definition

In telephone play, the telephone, as an instrument of play, is used in therapy to help facilitate communication.

ego may assume the role of the visible party while his or her self-image is projected onto the imagined second party, e.g., a child calls him- or herself on the phone, and, assuming the role of an adult, is reminded not to fear the doctor. For the child who can imagine conversations at both ends of the telephone, the therapeutic value of the telephone is immense.

Finally, the telephone can be helpful in dealing with a child's reluctance to talk in therapy. Spero writes about ten-year-old Billy, who sat through two intake sessions without speaking. It was suggested that he telephone the therapist and speak as his father, to try to convince the therapist to see "his son." Billy was also told that he could then call, as himself, to explain why he would rather not come to therapy. During the enactment of his father, Billy made such an effective case for consultation that he remained on the phone and, still playing his father, revealed important information about "his son."

Indicators/Measures of Success

When the child is willing and able to use the telephone as a means of expression, and the therapist gains valuable insight into the child's problems, this technique can be considered successful.

Suggested Readings and Resources

Miller, W. "The Telephone in Outpatient Psychotherapy." *American Journal of Psychotherapy*, 27: 15-26.

Spero, Moshe. "Use of the Telephone in Play Therapy." In Charles Schaefer and Donna Cangelosi, eds. *Play Therapy Technique* (Northvale, NJ: Jason Aronson, 1993).

Technique

The Therapist on the Inside

When to Use the Technique

Children who have problems such as sexualized behaviors, stealing, nighttime fears, or aggressiveness can be helped through the use of this intervention.

Patient Age and Profile

This technique works best when used with school-aged children. Younger children, for whom this situation may be too abstract, can draw the problem, then draw it again with the therapist directly involved and helping, then draw the problem after it is resolved.

How the Technique Works

After the therapist and child have established a rapport, the therapist says to the child, "You know me so well now. You know so much about the way I am with you, and you know the way you are with me. You know about the way I talk to you and how things go with us. You know how I think and feel about a lot of things now. You really have a lot of parts of me, and you and me together, on the inside of you now. How about if you pretend I'm right there with you and able to talk to you? I wonder if you can imagine what I might say to you. How might I help if I could be with you right then and there?" At this point, the therapist and child visualize the conversation and calm feelings that might ensue.

Grigoryev advises that this technique can also be used to foster internalization of other appropriate nurturing objects for the child, such as an appropriate new parent figure who is soothing and provides some structure and consistency in the child's life.

Indicators/Measures of Success

Grigoryev writes, "Behavioral acting out may reflect the loss to esteem that occurs when painful affects are experienced without inner regulation. The child can be benefited if he or she can find a way to access the memory of the soothing, regulating experience afforded by the

Definition

In this technique, developed by Patricia Grigoryev, the child is encouraged to directly evoke a memory of the therapist offering soothing and helpful support when the next problem is encountered. This is helpful in developing internal structures for self-regulation and an ability to tolerate negative situations.

therapist during face-to-face sessions. Gradually, attempts to internalize the therapist will lead to positive changes in the self. Over time, the internalization of good objects allows the self to become more cohesive and more self-sufficient" (pp. 366-67).

Suggested Readings and Resources

Grigoryev, Patricia. "The Therapist on the Inside." In Heidi Kaduson and Charles Schaefer, eds. *101 Favorite Play Therapy Techniques* (Northvale, NJ: Jason Aronson, 1997).

Technique

Token Economies

When to Use the Technique

Although a token system can be applied to an individual, the technique is generally used in group settings such as families, classrooms, psychiatric hospitals, or corrective facilities. Myles et al. (1992) emphasize that the technique should be undertaken "only when less intrusive measures" have failed.

Patient Age and Profile

Young elementary school-aged children respond to token economies, as do children who have developmental disabilities. The technique is often applied to children with aggressive or noncompliant behaviors.

How the Technique Works

Specific elements of the token economy must be planned. For example:

- target behaviors should be clear, observable, and measurable;

- reinforcers selected should appeal to the children;

- details about the token types, their distribution, and their redemption should enhance, rather than detract, from the main purpose of the group (academic instruction, safe play, etc.);

- after target behaviors are achieved, the system should eventually "fade" as participants rely less on intrusive reinforcers to motivate appropriate behavior.

Tokens can be distributed to individuals within the group, but they can also be applied to the group as an entity. A teacher's desk may display a canister into which he or she contributes marbles when the whole class behaves in a predetermined way (Thompson and Rudolph, 1996). A full canister then could buy the class a popcorn party.

Indicators/Measures of Success

Studies indicate that token economies work to reduce fighting and similar disruptive behaviors while they are being implemented, but that these behaviors return when the token system is withdrawn (Kazdin,

Definition

A token economy is a system of positive reinforcement that is built around the award of concrete tokens for appropriate behavior. A "contract" typically spells out for the parties involved how specific behavioral expectations are linked to rewards. The tokens (stickers, points, adult signatures, etc.) given for immediate reinforcement may be accumulated over time and later traded in for other rewards (special time, treats, privileges, etc.).

1985). There are concerns about the generalization of desired behaviors in other settings (Kazdin and Bootzin, 1972).

Suggested Readings and Resources

Kazdin, Alan. *Treatment of Antisocial Behavior in Children and Adolescents.* Homewood, Illinois: The Dorsey Press, 1985.

Kazdin, Alan., and R. Bootzin. "The Token Economy: An Evaluative Review." *Journal of Applied Behavior Analysis,* 5: 343-372.

Myles, B., M. Moran, C. Ormsbee, and J. Downing. "Guidelines for Establishing and Maintaining Token Economies." Intervention in School and Clinic, 27(3): 164-169. Also: http://www.cet.fsu.edu/tree/myles.html

Patterson, R. *Maintaining Effective Token Economies.* Springfield, Illinois: Charles Thomas, 1976.

Thompson, Charles, and Linda Rudolph. "Marbles for Auditory Reinforcement." In *Counseling Children* (Pacific Grove, CA: Brooks/Cole Publishing Company, 1996).

Technique

The Trifocal Model for Reversing Underachievement

When to Use the Technique

This technique can be used with the child who does not perform as well in school (typically as measured by grade average) as one would predict on the basis of certain tests or other measures of intelligence.

Patient Age and Profile

School-aged children as well as adolescents can be helped with this model.

How the Technique Works

Mandel and Marcus (1995) assert that the key to achievement is motivation, for which there is a very strict recipe, the ingredients of which are *vision, commitment, planning*, and *follow-through*. Each of these four ingredients is equally important, and each must be added in the correct order. In their discussion of underachievement, the authors maintain that every underachiever has "got stuck somewhere along the way while putting together this simple but unalterable recipe" (p. 18).

Rimm maintains that the underachieving child continues to underachieve because the home, school, and/or peer group support that underachievement. She writes, "Working below one's ability affects both immediate educational success and eventual career achievement; it is an important problem requiring attention." The steps in utilizing this model are as follows:

1. **Assessment.** The main purpose of this first step is to determine the extent and direction of a child's underachievement. Formal assessment measures include group or individual intelligence and achievement tests and creativity and underachievement inventories. Informal evaluations involve the questioning and observation of children by their parents and teachers.

2. **Communication.** Communication between parents and teachers is an important component in the reversal of underachievement. A parent or teacher may initiate the first conference, and the initiator must assure the other person of support, rather than placing blame. The parties should discuss the child's assessed abilities and achievements as well as

Definition

This six-step model was developed by Sylvia Rimm to treat underachieving children. Focusing on the child, the parents, and the school, it is based on the premise that because the characteristic behaviors of Underachievement Syndrome are learned, new behaviors, habits, and attitudes can also be learned.

evaluate the child's expressions of dependence or dominance.

3. **Changing expectations.** The expectations of parents, teachers, peers, siblings, and the underachievers themselves can be hard to change when low levels of performance have been the norm. "It is important to underachieving children that parents and teachers be able to tell them honestly that they believe in their ability to achieve," Davis and Rimm (1994) assert. "The expectations of these important others are basic to the personal change in self-expectations that is necessary to reverse from underachievement to high achievement" (p. 307).

4. **Role model identification.** A critical turning point for the underachieving child is the discovery of a model for identification. Davis and Rimm assert that "[a]ll of the treatments for underachievement dim in importance compared with strong identification with an achieving model" (p. 307). This person may be a tutor, mentor, companion, teacher, parent, sibling, counselor, psychologist, minister, scout leader, doctor, etc. The model should have as many of the following characteristics as possible: a strong sense of nurturance; similarities to the child, which may include same sex, religion, race, interests, talents, physical disabilities, physical characteristics, socioeconomic backgrounds, specific problem experiences, or any other characteristics that will create the necessary rapport; a sense of openness; a willingness to give time; and a sense of positive accomplishment.

5. **Correction of deficiencies.** Underachievers who are faring poorly in school may not have learned basic educational skills that are necessary for success. Davis and Rimm maintain that a tutorial system is most expedient for efficiently eliminating skill gaps, but caution that tutors should avoid fostering dependence, provide a goal-oriented framework for accomplishments, and move children through material as quickly as they can handle it.

6. **Specific interventions.** These include modifications of home and school reinforcements that support underachievement. Rewards can run the gamut from gold stars or extra art time to special outings with parents or monetary rewards. Considerations in determining rewards include the meaningfulness of the award to the child within the value system and range of possibility for the givers; the appropriate size of the reward (e.g., rewards should not be too large; in fact, they should be as small as possible, yet effective enough to motivate behavior); the ability of the reward to be increased in value; and the necessity for the reward always to be supplied as agreed upon.

Davis and Rimm write, "These recommendations for the treatment of underachievement at home and school are effective with many children and adolescents if the underachievement is not complicated by heavy involvement in drugs, alcohol, crime, or serious depression. However, even the adolescent who shows a long history of 'complicated' underachievement also may be able to reverse the underachieving pattern" (p. 310).

Indicators/Measures of Success

Sylvia Rimm has developed three instruments for the identification and assessment of underachieving students:

1. **Achievement Identification Measure (AIM).** This is an objective parent report of typical student behaviors that serves to standardize, objectify, and simplify information. It is helpful for communicating to parents the characteristics of their children's achievement motivation.

2. **Group Achievement Identification Measure (GAIM).** This is a self-report for preadolescents and teenagers (grades five-twelve). It permits students to describe their own behaviors and attitudes and quantifies students' self-perceptions, comparing them to a national norm.

3. **Achievement Identification Measure-Teacher Observation (AIM-TO).** This is a teacher observation instrument to be used for students in grades one through twelve. It is especially useful when a team of teachers want to share their observations of a child.

These tools are available from the Educational Assessment Service, Inc., W6050 Apple Road, Watertown, WI 53098-3937 (1-800-795-7466).

Suggested Readings and Resources

Davis, G., and Sylvia Rimm. "Underachievement: Diagnosis and Treatment." In *Education of the Gifted and Talented* (Boston: Allyn & Bacon, 1994).

Mandel, Harvey, Sander Marcus, and Dorothy Mandel. *Helping the Non-achievement Syndrome Student.* Toronto: The Institute on Achievement and Motivation, 1992.

Rimm, Sylvia. *Underachievement Syndrome: Causes and Cures.* Watertown, WI: Apple Publishing Co., 1986.

_____. *Why Bright Kids Get Poor Grades (and What You Can Do About It).* New York: Crown Publishers, 1995.

Urine Alarm Training

When to Use the Technique

This technique is used for enuresis (bedwetting) after medical problems have been ruled out. Because enuresis is associated with many factors, this technique is often used in conjunction with a program of other interventions.

Patient Age and Profile

Therapists use this technique for children ages five to fourteen.

How the Technique Works

Families should expect to work with this technique consistently for two to four months and are encouraged to plan travel or other interruptions around this block of time.

The apparatus works because the saline content of the urine on the pad completes an electrical circuit linking the pad to the alarm. Advocates of the technique attest to its safety.

The process demands that the child take increased responsibility for solving the problem. The technique is explained to the child, and the child sets the alarm him- or herself. The child is encouraged to sleep without pajama bottoms for convenience and efficiency. During the night, when the child begins to urinate, the buzzer will ring, and the child is supposed to shut it off and go to the bathroom to complete urination. The child helps change the sheets and resets the buzzer. Parents are expected to cooperate by making sure that the child is fully awake, turning on the lights to complete the effect, and, depending on the age of the child, helping with the linen.

It is not altogether clear why the process works, but Schaefer believes the constant nighttime awakening process is aversive enough that the child becomes more sensitive to pressure in the bladder and strengthens the sphincter muscles to prevent accidental urination.

Indicators/Measures of Success

If there is no progress over the weeks of treatment, the technique should

Definition

Urine alarm training, also known as bell-and-pad conditioning, involves an electrical apparatus designed to stop children from bedwetting. Although the mechanical device has advanced since it was originally presented by Pfaundler in 1904 and revised in 1938 by Mowrer and Mowrer (Schaefer, 1997), it is set up so that the child sleeps over a pad that is connected to a buzzer. When urine touches the pad, the alarm sounds.

be stopped. One should expect that urination in bed will gradually diminish, that it will occur less frequently, and that the child will learn to "beat the bell" to the toilet. The pad and alarm may be removed after fourteen consecutive dry nights.

Relapse rates are very high, with weekly wetting in the first six months following treatment at about 30-40 percent. Overlearning [see pp. 110] is supposed to reduce relapse to the 20 percent range. Schaefer indicates that waiting for twenty-eight consecutive dry nights during the training, rather than the original target of fourteen, before removing the pad and bell contributes to greater success. One accident during this period of time is considered within the parameters of success.

Suggested Readings and Resources

Schaefer, Charles. *Childhood Encopresis and Enuresis: Causes and Therapy.* Northvale, N.J.: Jason Aronson, 1997.

The "When-Then" Strategy

When to Use the Technique

This short-term play therapy strategy is effective with disruptive children.

Patient Age and Profile

School-aged children can be helped through this technique.

How the Technique Works

Disruptive children can become resistant or overstimulated or go off-task during therapist-directed activities. To be efficient in accomplishing goals in short-term therapy, a therapist must deal with off-task and oppositional behaviors in a timely manner. To make the "When-Then" strategy work, the therapist should be careful to make the consequence more rewarding than what the child is already doing. As there is much variation in the degree of reinforcement that children will derive from different activities and rewards, the therapist must tailor the consequences to fit the individual child. For situations that involve a transition to a less pleasant activity, a tangible reinforcer can be incorporated into the strategy (e.g., "When you sit next to me, then I will put a sticker in your sticker book").

Other "When-Then" statements for encouraging cooperation include:

- When you take my hand, then I will open the door.

- When you ask me nicely, then I will hand you the marker.

- When you sit in the chair, then I will give you a snack.

- When you use your indoor voice, then you can take a turn.

- When you put the clay back in the can, then we can show this picture to your grandfather.

- When you are done with your bathroom break, then we can play with some new toys.

- When you show me how you relax your hands and arms, then we can take our break.

- When you tell me one more story, then we can get out the paints.

> ### Definition
>
> The "When-Then" strategy is most commonly used in play therapy when a child has failed to comply with a direction, is dawdling, or has begun a minor disruptive behavior. Children are told that a pleasant, rewarding activity will be provided once they engage in a specific behavior. The therapist states the contingency by saying something like, "When you practice how to handle teasing one more time, then we can use our colored chalk on the chalkboard."

- When you use your words to show me you are angry, then we can play what you want to play.

- When you ask me in your big-girl voice, then I will answer your question.

- When you play gently with the toys, then I will turn back around and play with you.

Indicators/Measures of Success

Success in using this technique depends on using rewards to serve as positive and viable alternatives to power struggles and confrontational management strategies. The best reward programs provide immediate gratification for specific behaviors, such as in the above examples. Observation of changes in behavior signals the successful use of the technique.

Suggested Readings and Resources

Bodiford-McNeil, Cheryl, Toni Hembree-Kigin, and Sheila Eyberg. *Short-Term Play Therapy for Disruptive Children.* Plainview, NY: Childswork/Childsplay, 1996.

Working with Parents: A Collaborative Model

When to Use the Technique

This model is effective when all of the significant adults in a child's life are willing to collaborate toward ameliorating the child's conduct disorder problems.

Patient Age and Profile

Children as young as three years of age can be aggressive, defiant, and noncompliant and thus benefit from this model.

How the Technique Works

Based on a combination of problem-oriented and humanistic therapy models, the authors' collaborative model emphasizes a reciprocal relationship in which parents and professionals share their knowledge and perspectives in designing an intervention. Rather than being a hierarchical relationship, in which a parent is seen as having deficits requiring intervention by a professional therapist, it is a process based on trust for working with parents of conduct-disordered children and for establishing a "nonblaming, supportive relationship based on using equally the therapist's knowledge and the parents' unique strengths and perspectives" (Webster-Stratton and Herbert, 1993).

In his or her role as collaborator, the therapist should listen to the parent, clarify issues, and teach and suggest alternatives. This model is intended to promote self-efficacy for parents, at a time when they may be very vulnerable (Christenson et al., 1997). In other words, parents need to be assisted in gaining knowledge and competence to cope effectively with the stress of having a conduct-disordered child. The primary missions of the therapist are as follows:

1. **Building a supportive relationship.** Using self-disclosure, humor, optimism, and advocacy for parents.

2. **Empowering parents.** Reinforcing and validating parents' insights, modifying powerless thoughts, promoting self-empowerment, building family/group support systems.

> ### Definition
>
> Carolyn Webster-Stratton and Martin Herbert (1994) have developed this collaborative model in which school professionals intervene concurrently with the parents and teachers of conduct-disordered children.

3. **Teaching.** Persuading, explaining, suggesting and adapting; giving assignments; reviewing and summarizing; ensuring generalization; providing videotape modeling examples; using role play and rehearsal; evaluating.

4. **Interpreting.** Using analogies and metaphors, reframing.

5. **Leading and challenging.** Setting limits, pacing the group, dealing with resistance.

6. **Prophesying.** Anticipating problems and setbacks, predicting parent resistance to change; predicting positive change/success.

Indicators/Measures of Success

The authors write, "Quantitative accounts of [our] Parenting Clinic's intervention programs…have shown that our programs are effective in promoting more positive parent-child interactional behaviors and in reducing child conduct disorders, as well as promoting more positive parental attitudes, in comparison to untreated control families and families who received only the parent group discussion treatment."

Suggested Readings and Resources

Christenson, Sandra, Julie Hirsch, and Christine Hurley. "Families with Aggressive Children and Adolescents." In Arnold Goldstein and Jane Conoley, eds. *School Violence Intervention: A Practical Handbook* (New York: The Guilford Press, 1997).

Webster-Stratton, Carolyn, and Martin Herbert. *Troubled Families—Problem Children.* New York: John Wiley & Sons, 1994.

—————————————————. "What Really Happens in Parent Training?" *Behavior Modification,* 17(4): 407-456.

The Worry List

When to Use the Technique

This technique is effective when a child has exhausted his or her intuitive capacity to solve a problem and feels overwhelmed by worry, fear, or anxiety.

Patient Age and Profile

The approach works best for children who feel flooded by strong emotions. There need not be a primary diagnosis of anxiety disorder.

How the Technique Works

The Worry List uses the magical imperatives and directives derived from the work of Milton Erickson (Haley, 1973) and incorporates the direct, educational approach of cognitive behaviorism (Meichenbaum, 1974). Sloves (1997) writes, "When vague, ethereal, intangible, or abstract experiences are concretized, they are more easily brought under conscious control...Once fears and worries are actually placed on the table, they are more easily examined, manipulated, reworked, and refashioned."

Here are the important aspects of the technique:

- Children are helped to identify what worries them. If they have trouble expressing themselves, diagnostic play or art therapy materials are used to illustrate or dramatize their concerns.

- The therapist keeps track of each explicit or implicit worry, fear, or concern. He or she develops the list in front of the child. Younger children may be helped with colorful drawings, and older children can be told, "These things are private. At the end of the session you can decide to put them in a special folder or to throw them in the trash can."

- The entire process should resemble a brainstorming process. Judgments of the items on the list are not made, and prioritizing comes later. Sloves writes, "We want to disassemble an overbearing concern into more manageable component parts." As well, ideas should be phrased in a way children can recognize as familiar: "Didn't you tell me something about how you feel when your mom comes home late from work?"

> ### Definition
>
> The Worry List involves devising a list of things that worry a child and then charting a "plan of attack" against them. Children are helped to label, concretize, and manipulate a particular subset of worries.

- The technique works best when the list contains at least five, but not more than ten, concerns.

- Something concrete (and psychologically correct) must be done with the worry.

Worries can be stored in a folder in a desk drawer to be discussed one at a time, as the child chooses. Sloves suggests variations, such as putting each worry in its own sealed envelope, or for younger children, building a fort and putting one worry in each room, and then telling the child, "Each worry is locked (sealed) inside its own strong room (envelope) and it can only come out when you decide to unlock (open) the door (flap) and let it out. So, if you're taking a math test or doing something important like that it won't come out and bother you."

Indicators/Measures of Success

With this technique, children are not asked to ignore or forget their concerns, but rather to pick the time and place to experience what they have previously avoided. In a calm atmosphere, children experience finite, planned doses of anxiety without their anticipated negative consequences. Studies have shown that children can be successfully trained in the effective use of psychological defense and how to use language and imagery to shape the problem-solving process.

Suggested Readings and Resources

Haley, Jay. *Uncommon Therapy: The Psychiatric Techniques of Milton Erickson, M.D.* New York: Norton, 1973.

Meichenbaum, Donald. *Cognitive-Behavior Modification.* New York: Plenum Press, 1974.

Sloves, Richard. "The Worry List." In Heidi Kaduson and Charles Schaefer, eds. *101 Favorite Play Therapy Techniques* (Northvale, N.J.: Jason Aronson, 1997).

Sloves, Richard, and K. Peterlin. "Time-Limited Play Therapy with Children." In Charles Schaefer and Kevin O'Connor, eds. *Handbook of Play Therapy: Vol. II* (New York: John Wiley & Sons, 1994).

Wraparound

One of Wraparound's fundamental premises is that children function and mature best in the most "natural" environment. This means going to regular schools, living at home (or in a long-term foster family or adoptive family), playing, socializing, and attending extracurricular activities in the community. With everyone on a team agreeing to "never give up," a child or adolescent has more than a fighting chance of eventually being able to cope in his or her environment.

When to Use the Technique

Chronically dysfunctional families or families in crisis can benefit most from this program.

Patient Age and Profile

Children from birth to age twenty-one can be served through this intervention.

How the Technique Works

Some examples of the types of services available through Wraparound are intensive one-to-one interventions in community settings, behavioral consultations, "mobile" psychotherapy, creative arts therapies, and school-based interventions. The International Initiative on the Development, Training, and Evaluation of Wraparound Services offers the following explanation of the components of Wraparound:

- **It is developed and/or approved by an interdisciplinary services team.** This team, at a minimum, includes:

  1. The parent and/or surrogate parent (e.g., foster parent or guardian);

  2. If the child is in custody, the appropriate representative of the state (social worker or probation officer);

  3. A lead teacher and/or vocational counselor;

  4. If the child is in mental health treatment or should be in mental health treatment, the appropriate therapist or counselor;

  5. A case manager or services coordinator (the person who is responsible for ensuring that the services are coordinated and

Definition

The Wraparound process is a way to improve the lives of children and families who have complex needs. An individualized model that is designed around each child's own circumstances, it seeks to create supports that can help a child and his or her family stay in the community and function adequately there. Wraparound is usually sponsored by a broad-based coalition of local agencies and service providers.

accountable);

6. An advocate of the child and/or parent;

7. Any other person influential in the child's or parents' life who may be instrumental in developing effective services, such as a neighbor, a physician, a relative, or a friend; and

8. The child, unless to do so would be detrimental to his or her development.

- **It is community-based in the local community or rural area where the child and his or her family live.** Restrictive or institutional care should be accessed for brief stabilization only.

- **It is unconditional.** The team agrees to change services as needs of the child and family change, never to deny services because of extreme severity of disability, and never to reject the child or family from services.

- **It is centered on the strengths of the child and family.** The positive aspects of the child, family, and community must be considered and must be part of individualized services.

- **It includes coordinated, highly individualized services.** These are based on specific needs of the child and/or family, and not on a particular categorical intervention model. These individualized services are both traditional (therapy, foster care, etc.) and nontraditional (hiring a "special" friend, bringing staff to live in a family home, providing special recreational services, etc.). Traditional services should be accessed only when they can be tailored to the specific needs of the child and family.

- **It considers life domain needs.** These are areas of basic human needs that almost everyone experiences. They are:

1. residential (a place to live);

2. family or surrogate family;

3. social (friends and contact with other people);

4. educational and/or vocational;

5. medical;

6. psychological/emotional;

7. legal (especially for children with juvenile justice needs);

8. safety (the need to be safe); and

9. cultural/ethnic needs, community needs, etc.

Indicators/Measures of Success

In their comprehensive report, *One Kid at a Time* (1993), John Burchard, Sara Burchard, Robert Sewell, and John VanDenBerg detail the results of the Alaska Youth Initiative (AYI) Demonstration Project, a five-year program that focused on ten youths with severe behavioral and emotional problems, including borderline personality, conduct disorder, depression, substance abuse, ADHD, possible multiple personality, and schizophrenia. The authors write, "An essential component of the success of AYI was fitting the services to the youth rather than trying to fit the youth to a program."

In the AYI Wraparound project, one youth was placed in a twenty-four-hour-staffed apartment rather than a group home, one was provided a paid friend for social integration, another youth lived in an apartment with an admired mentor or peer, and another lived with a young couple and their child in order to learn parenting skills.

The best youth outcomes were associated with providers whose attitude reflected unconditional care "no matter what the kid does." In general, staff stayed with the youth, retrieved the youth, negotiated with the youth, and stood up for the youth through the most difficult times. Through this process, they developed mutual, trusting relationships that helped to minimize the multiple placement shuffle.

At the end of the project, it was reported that eight of the youths were now young adults living successfully in the community. All but one were living fairly independently, having gained significantly in self-respect and confidence concerning their future. "They had gained personal empowerment," the authors write, "[and] had acquired many skills: skills in daily living, skills in self-control, some educational and work-related skills, skills for finding and using assistance from social programs, and skills in accessing community resources." Those with serious drug dependencies appeared to have broken their drug habits. They had also built the beginnings of meaningful social support networks.

The two youngest of the ten remained in specialized foster homes, also having gained enormously in self-control, self-respect, and social skills. They had access to activities and opportunities within the mainstream culture that would eventually empower them to succeed as adults.

Suggested Readings and Resources

Burchard, J., S. Burchard, R. Sewell, and J. VanDenBerg. *One Kid At a Time: Evaluative Case Studies and Description of The Alaska Youth Initiative Demonstration Project.* Washington, DC: Georgetown University Child Development Center, 1993.

VanDenBerg, J. "Children Need Individualized Services." *NAMI Advocate,* 12:4, 5.